11+ C.E.M. Style test

Set A: Paper 1

GW01451789

Read the following instructions carefully:
1. Do not open this booklet until told to do so.
2. You must answer the questions on the answer sheet provided.
3. You may do any rough working on a separate sheet of paper.
4. This test consists of five separately timed sections. You must not go on to the next section until you are told to do so.
5. Follow the instructions at the bottom of each page.
6. If you do make a mistake rub it out and put in your new answer.
7. Do not spend too long on a question, if a question is taking a long time move on to the next.
8. If you do not know the answer to the question, choose the answer you think best.
9. Not all sections have a time warning.
10. If you finish a section early you may go back and review any questions that are within the section that you are working on only. You must wait for further instructions before moving onto another section. You may not move back to a previous section.

Copyright © achieve2day   2015

Published by achieve2day, Slough.

Example

Read the passage below then answer the questions that follow:

Ypres

Ypres is an agricultural town in Belgium. It has a long history and has been the site of many battles, since the Romans conquered Ypres in 58-50BC. Ypres came to prominence in the Middle Ages as a place where cloth was bought and sold. The large Cloth Hall was built between 1260 and 1304. Unfortunately, the town was completely destroyed during the First World War. The beautiful buildings including the magnificent Cloth Hall and the cathedral were reconstructed in the original medieval style after the war. Today it is common place for secondary school students to visit Ypres on history trips, the Cloth Hall now a war museum and tourist centre.

    i.   According to the author, what is ***not*** true of the current Cloth Hall at Ypres?
        A.   It was built in the medieval ages.
        B.   It now houses a war museum.
        C.   It is very large.
        D.   It is in a medieval style.

According to the passage the buildings were reconstructed after being destroyed in the war. Therefore, while the original Cloth Hall was built in the Medieval Ages, the current one was not. Therefore the answer is A.

Comprehension
Read the passage below then answer the questions that follow:

Christmas Island

Christmas Island, now infamous as the location of a detention centre for refugees, is an island full of natural wonders.

Christmas Island is located in the Indian Ocean, south of Indonesia and north-west of Australia. It is a small island with an area not much more than a third of the area of the Isle of Wight. The population of 2000 residents live in settlement areas while almost two thirds of the island has been declared a National Park.

The Blowholes are a geological feature located along the limestone cliff in the south of the island. The Blowholes are holes in the ground. As a result of waves crashing into caves formed along the bottom of the cliffs, water and trapped air are forced out of the holes leading to spectacular plumes of water.

The island has a large number of animals that are endemic to the island. There are five types of mammal on the island, all of them small, of which only one is an endemic species. However, there are many types of unique birds, reptiles and invertebrates. The islands most renowned creature is the Christmas Island Red Crab. The Red Crab has an annual breeding migration, of millions of individuals, which has been described by David Attenborough as one of the natural wonders of the world. The Red Crab which is normally bright red in colour has a number of habitats including domestic gardens but their highest density is in the rainforest. The island also has seventeen unique plant species.

The people of the island are no less interesting. The diversity of the settlers has created the islands unique, vibrant culture and range of festivals that are held throughout the year.

1. According to the passage, Christmas Island is:
   A. Purely positive
   B. A land of contrasts
   C. One of the natural wonders of the world
   D. Small and insignificant

Go on to the next page.

2. Blowholes are:
    A. Holes in limestone
    B. Jets of water spraying high into the air
    C. Limestone caves
    D. The South coast

3. In the passage the word endemic means:
    A. Very uncommon
    B. Found nowhere else
    C. Animals that migrate
    D. Very common

4. From the passage, which statement could **not** be true of the red crabs?
    A. Rarely seen
    B. Most are red but some are purple
    C. There are estimated to be 120 million on the island
    D. They migrate each Spring to the Ocean

5. What is a possible reason for the Island's name?
    A. It is near the North Pole
    B. It was discovered on Christmas Day
    C. Elves live there
    D. Large reindeer roam the Island

6. Where could this article be found?
    A. In a newspaper
    B. In a novel
    C. In an encyclopaedia
    D. In an atlas

7. An invertebrate is?
    A. An animal without a backbone
    B. A plant
    C. A type of fungi
    D. A fish

8. The word diversity means:
    A. positive
    B. a range of different things
    C. lots
    D. better than the surroundings

Do NOT go on to the next page until told to do so.

Examples

Complete the words in capitals in the passage below.

i.   The boy was very excited that it was his birthday and was hoping to
         RE☐☐☐VE lots of presents.

The word is receive, so the missing letters are C,E,I, in that order.

ODD ONE OUT

Three of the words in each list are connected in the same way. Mark the word which is not related to the other three.

ii.: uncle, grandfather, niece, nephew.
Answer: niece (all the others are male)

Complete the words in capitals, in the passage below.

Post-it notes

Sometimes apparent failures can result in amazing discoveries. In 1968 Dr Silver was working at 3M ¹LAB☐☐☐TORIES in America. He was trying to develop a super-strong ²AD☐☐☐IVE, to be used in building planes. Instead, he ³AC☐☐DENT☐☐LY created a weak, ⁴REU☐☐☐LE glue. Silver promoted his product within the company for five years, but with no success. Art Fry, an engineer at 3M, sang in his church ⁵C☐☐☐R. He was continually having the problem of losing page markers in the hymnal. He decided that 3M should put Silver's glue on pieces of paper that would temporarily stick to anything. As a result in 1980 Post-it notes went on sale. Ten years later they were recognised as one of the top ⁶CONS☐☐☐R products of the decade.

Odd One Out

Three of the words in each list are connected in the same way. Mark the word which is not related to the other three.

7.	Spain	France	Hungary	Japan
8.	potato	apple	grape	mango
9.	whale	manatee	gecko	meerkat
10.	train	car	plain	ship
11.	filthy	stingy	dirty	grimy
12.	reduce	demolish	diminish	decrease
13.	pledge	prize	award	trophy
14.	strict	stern	husky	stringent
15.	tune	anthem	composer	hymn
16.	listen	tinsel	silent	hear

Do NOT go on to the next page until told to do so.

Example

Work out which set of blocks can be put together to make the figure on the left.

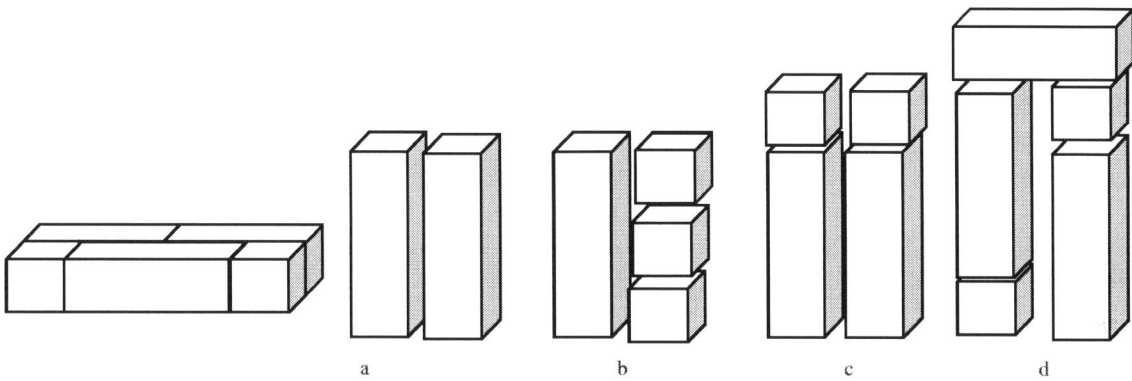

a   b   c   d

Answer: d

Do not go on until told to do so.

1.

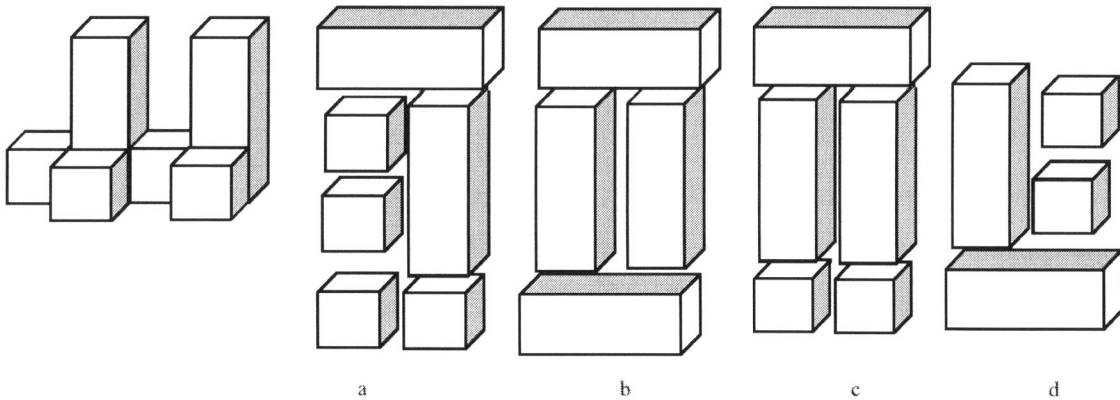

a   b   c   d

Go on to the next page.

2.

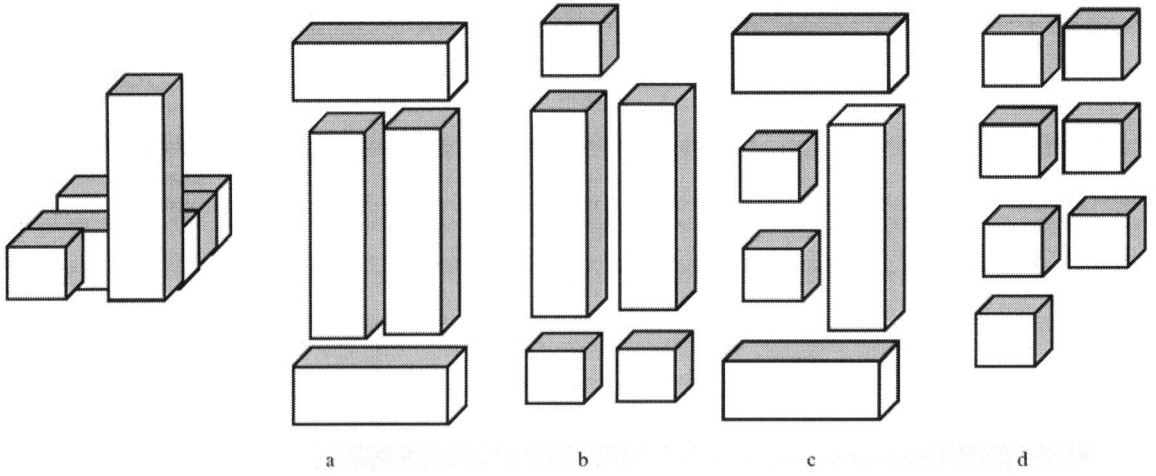

a   b   c   d

3.

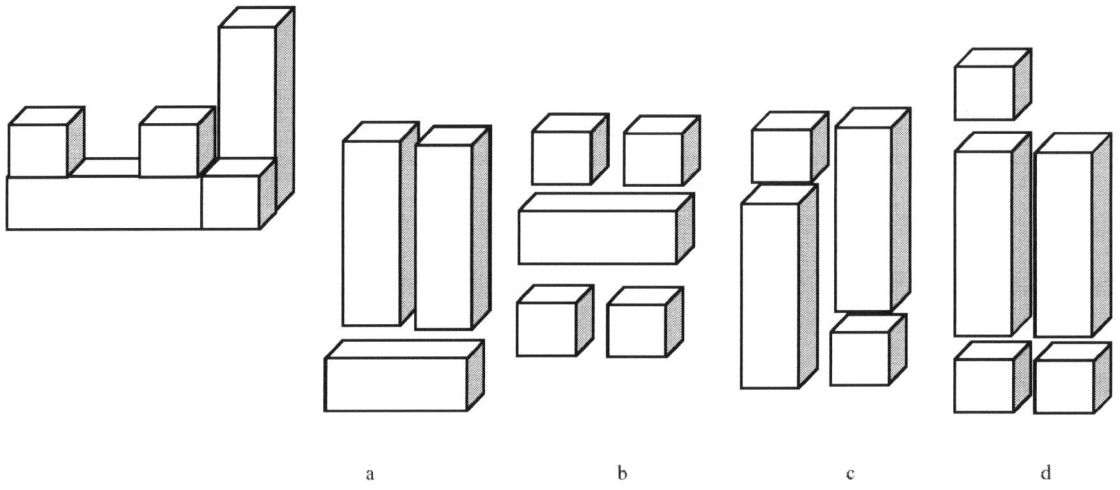

a   b   c   d

4.

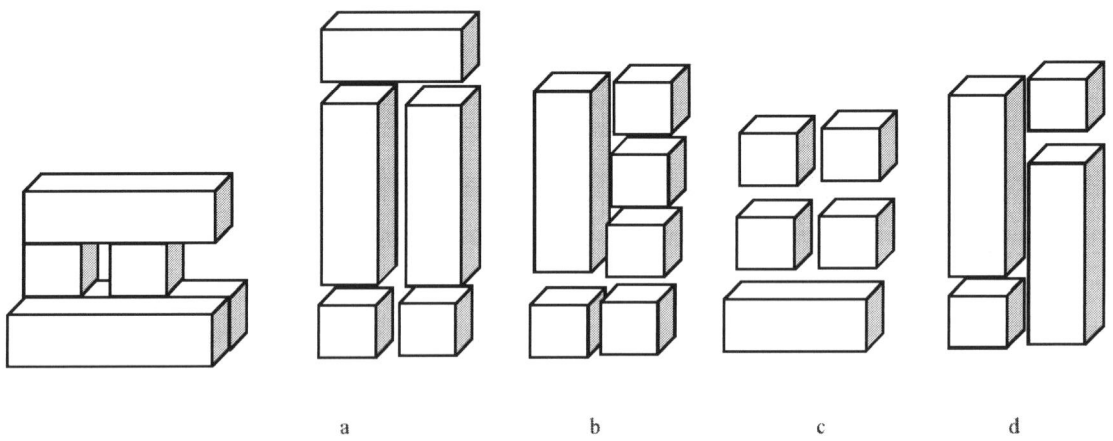

a   b   c   d

Go on to the next page.

Work out which shape has been rotated to make the given shape.

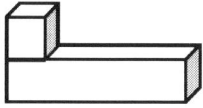
a

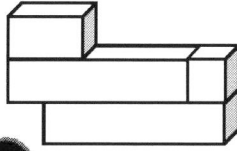
b

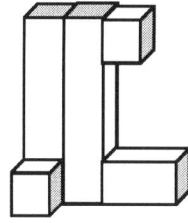
c

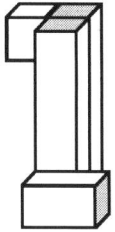
d

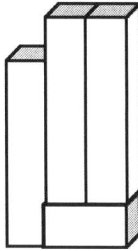
e

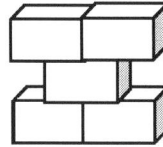
f

5.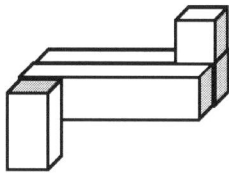

a ☐   d ☐

b ☐   e ☐

c ☐   f ☐

6.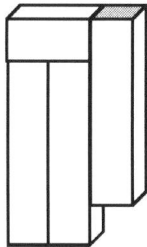

a ☐   d ☐

b ☐   e ☐

c ☐   f ☐

7.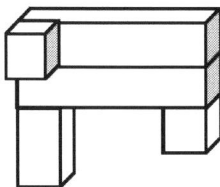

a ☐   d ☐

b ☐   e ☐

c ☐   f ☐

Do NOT go on to the next page until told to do so.

Example

In the questions below: Work out which cube can be made by folding the net on the left.

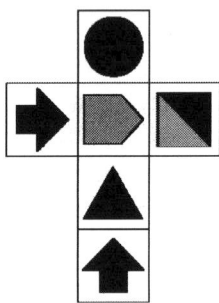
   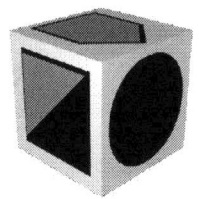

A.   B.   C.   D.

The answer is C.

1.

    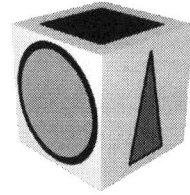

A.   B.   C.   D.

2.

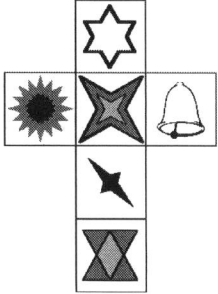 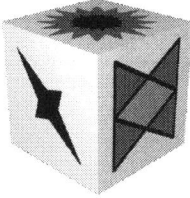  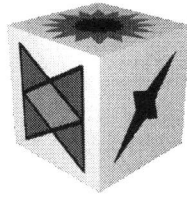 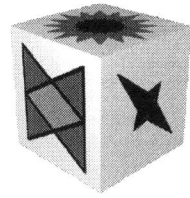

A.   B.   C.   D.

3.

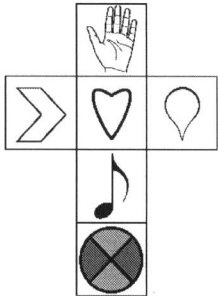 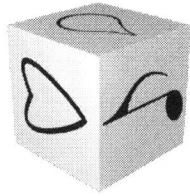  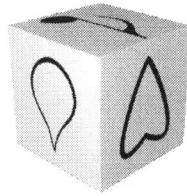 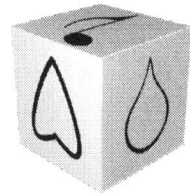

A.   B.   C.   D.

4.

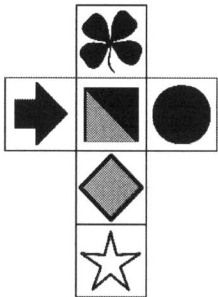    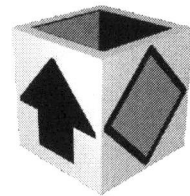

A.   B.   C.   D.

5.

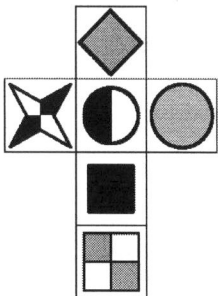    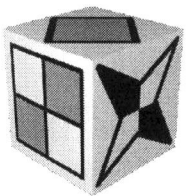

A.   B.   C.   D.

Go on to the next page.

6.

    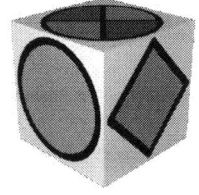

         A.   B.   C.   D.

7.

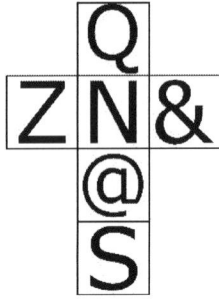    

         A.   B.   C.   D.

8.

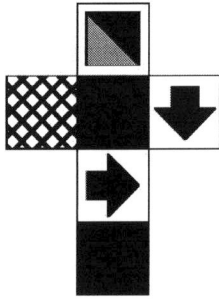 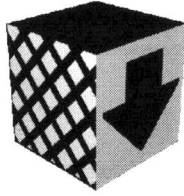 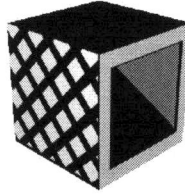  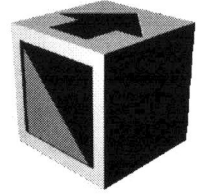

         A.   B.   C.   D.

9.

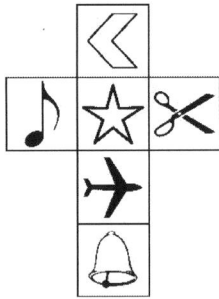 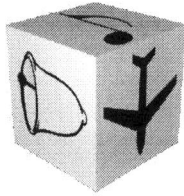 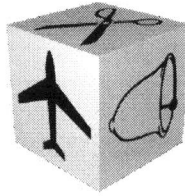  

         A.   B.   C.   D.

10.

 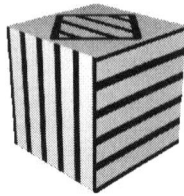  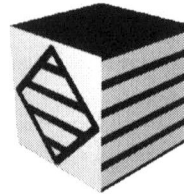 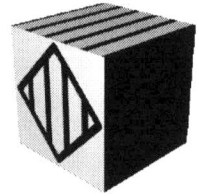

         A.   B.   C.   D.

Do NOT go on to the next page until told to do so.

Examples

i. Find the area of the rectangle below:

20cm	
	2.1cm

Answer: 42 cm²

ii. Subtract 3mm from 8cm. Give your answer in cm.

Answer: 7.7cm

i.

0	4	2	cm²
[0]	[0]	[0]	
[1]	[1]	[1]	
[2]	[2]	[2]	
[3]	[3]	[3]	
[4]	[4]	[4]	
[5]	[5]	[5]	
[6]	[6]	[6]	
[7]	[7]	[7]	
[8]	[8]	[8]	
[9]	[9]	[9]	

ii.

7	.	7	cm
[0]	.	[0]	
[1]	.	[1]	
[2]	.	[2]	
[3]	.	[3]	
[4]	.	[4]	
[5]	.	[5]	
[6]	.	[6]	
[7]	.	[7]	
[8]	.	[8]	
[9]	.	[9]	

Do NOT go on to the next page until told to do so.

1. 374 + 68 + 237

2. 613 − 287

3. $\frac{5}{8}$ of 320

4. Amy is baking and uses 750g of flour from a 2.5 kg bag. How many kilograms of flour are left?

5. Emily leaves home at 7:50 a.m.. She has a 15 minute walk to the train station and then catches the 8:22 a.m. train. How long does she wait at the train station?

6. Three trains leave from Fenchurch Street Station. Train A leaves every 3 minutes, train B every 5 minutes and train C every 8 minutes to Monopoly Street Station. The first train of the day is at 6:00 a.m. for all three trains. What time of the day do they next leave the station together?

Go on to the next page.

The next two questions use the following information:
Josh, Jake, Ian and Paul are making a poster. They have 12, 7, 19 and 26 pens respectively.

7.   What is the average number of pens?

8. A fifth person, Steven, asks to help and they agree. When they add in Steven's felt tips the average number of pens is 18. How many pens does Steven have?

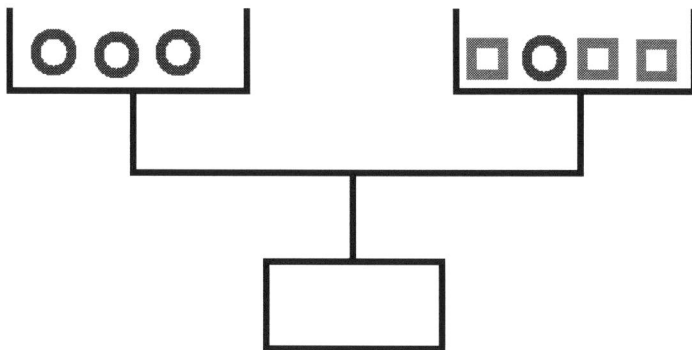

9. If each ⬤ has a mass of 30g, what is the mass of each ▣?

10. A School of 1210 students go to a Christmas pantomime. If each coach can seat 50 students, how many coaches are needed for the trip?

11. A square has a perimeter of 24 cm. What is the area of the square?

Go on to the next page.

12. Below is a pie chart of raw materials used by a factory, in a week. It is shown in percentage by weight.

copper=25
lead=50
wood=12.5
glass=12.5
sand=50
cement=50

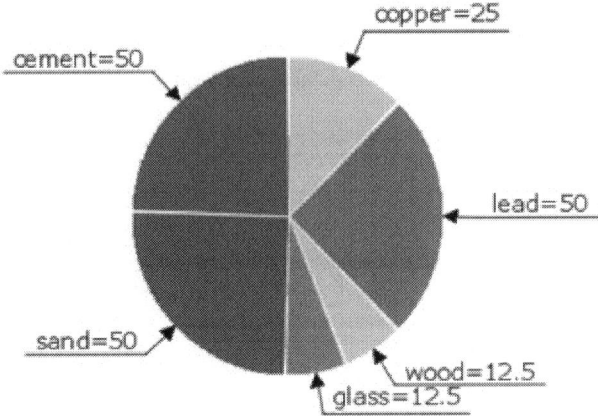

cement=50

copper=25

lead=50

sand=50

wood=12.5

glass=12.5

The factory uses 2 kg of copper each week. If the cost of lead is £1.50 per kg how much does the factory spend on lead each week?

11+ C.E.M. Style test

Set A: Paper 2

Read the following instructions carefully:

1. Do not open this booklet until told to do so.
2. You must answer the questions on the answer sheet provided.
3. You may do any rough working on a separate sheet of paper.
4. This test consists of four separately timed sections. You must not go on to the next section until you are told to do so.
5. Follow the instructions at the bottom of each page.
6. If you do make a mistake rub it out and put in your new answer.
7. Do not spend too long on a question, if a question is taking a long time move on to the next.
8. If you do not know the answer to the question, choose the answer you think best.
9. Not all sections have a time warning.
10. If you finish a section early you may go back and review any questions that are within the section that you are working on only. You must wait for further instructions before moving onto another section. You may not move back to a previous section.

Copyright © achieve2day 2015

Published by achieve2day, Slough.

Example

Read the passage below then answer the questions that follow:

Joshua's Favourite Day

Friday was Joshua's favourite day of the week. Not just because it was the day before the week-end, but because it was the day that he got to take his friend's dragon for a walk at the local park. It had taken him a long time to gain the trust of the dragon. Nevertheless, now that he had befriended the dragon and they had trained him, Fridays were the day that he looked forward to even more than Saturdays.

   i.   What was Joshua's favourite day of the Week?
  A. Sunday.
  B. Monday.
  C. Wednesday.
  D. Friday.
  E. Saturday.

According to the passage Friday was Joshua's favourite day of the week. Therefore the answer is D.

Read the article below, then answer the following questions.

THE DAILY TIMES

www.achieve2day.com   **Current events**   £0.60

Local Artist Frances Parish's art show at Slough's West Wing Art Centre.

Contemporary portrait artist Frances Parish creates memories and tells stories on canvas. Using acrylic paint, brushes, palette knives and occasionally her fingers, Mrs. Parish captures images from around the world. Mrs. Parish's one-woman show opens in the Blue Room at the West Wing Art Centre on Stoke Road at 7.00 pm on Saturday, 23rd May. Mrs. Parish, who prefers to be called "Francie," says of her upcoming show, "Some images may be confronting to some people, as so many things that we take for granted in the UK such as clean water are not available in many places."

However, she is quick to point out that equally there are many uplifting images demonstrating the generosity and resilience of the human spirit.

Francie began painting pictures in her teens, when her grandmother signed her up for a summer workshop. Firmly captivated with the process of drawing and painting, Francie pursued formal training, graduating Summa Cum Laud from the National College of Art and Design in Dublin, Ireland, obtaining a Bachelor's Degree in Fine Art. Francie continued to study and develop her signature style using gouache paint, at a small private atelier and later opened her own studio.

Over the years she has experimented with and worked in watercolour pencils, watercolour, gouache and acrylic—which is her primary medium.

1. How many types of paint does Francie use?
   a. 1
   b. 2
   c. 3
   d. 4
   e. 5

Go on to the next page.

2. How does Francie think the public will view her work?
    a. Depressing.
    b. Uplifting.
    c. Emotional – both depressing and uplifting.
    d. Pretty.
    e. Make them think about water.

3. What is the main purpose of this article?
    a. Inform.
    b. Entertain.
    c. Persuade.
    d. Make people think about other places.
    e. Advertise.

4. What does the word "atelier" mean?
    a. An experienced artist or craftsman.
    b. An artist's studio.
    c. A school.
    d. A suburb or area of Paris.
    e. A person who no longer paints but teaches others the craft.

5. Where did Francie go to College?
    a. England.
    b. Wales.
    c. Scotland.
    d. Ireland.
    e. United States of America.

6. Where does Francie live?
    a. Slough.
    b. London.
    c. Dublin.
    d. West Wing.
    e. Doesn't say.

7. What type of word is resilience?
    a. Noun.
    b. Verb.
    c. Adjective.
    d. Adverb.
    e. Article.

Example:

Opposites
Complete the opposite of the word below.

   i.   above   b☐l☐☐

Answer: e,o,w (the word is below).

Extra Word
In these questions the words of a sentence are jumbled up with an extra word added. Determine what the sentence is, then find the word that remains.

   ii.   flat battery start end car wouldn't because the the was

Answer: end (the sentence is: The car wouldn't start because the battery was flat).

Opposites
Complete the opposite of the words below.

1. ordered   r☐nd☐☐

2. floor   ☐☐☐ling

3. abundant   ☐p☐☐☐e

4. crazy   s☐☐☐

5. reality   ☐anta☐☐

6. trap   ☐el☐☐se

7. agreement   ☐on☐☐ict

8. frenzied   ☐ere☐☐

9. bold   t☐☐☐d

10. blunt   t☐☐☐ful

11. dye   bl☐☐☐h

12. former   la☐t☐☐

13. proud   ☐☐m☐le

14. virtuous   ☐orr☐☐t

Go on to the next page.

Extra Word

In these questions the words of a sentence are jumbled up with an extra word added. Determine what the sentence is, then find the word that remains.

15. it is practice day piano good to the everyday

16. hurts to singing throat sore my

17. you brush teeth twice should your times everyday

18. forecast the weather day hot it would be said

19. Paris the capital France of is was

20. caused crops to not grow late frost the to well

21. stood up bus timetable for elderly people always on the she

22. on sorting classification is groups things into

23. treat treated others likes you would like to be as

24. the Sun Earth rotates it around every year once the

25. speech he long the was monotonous and very

26. so it a day walk beautiful was a decided go they to for holidays

27. applied shop job he local for at a the checkouts part-time

28. day diary many keep journal people a or

29. snowed hazardous conditions it heavily night causing driving

30. before buy the ran just he to closing shops time

Do NOT go on to the next page until told to do so.

Examples:

To the left of each line are five squares. Find which square on the right completes the series on the left.

i.

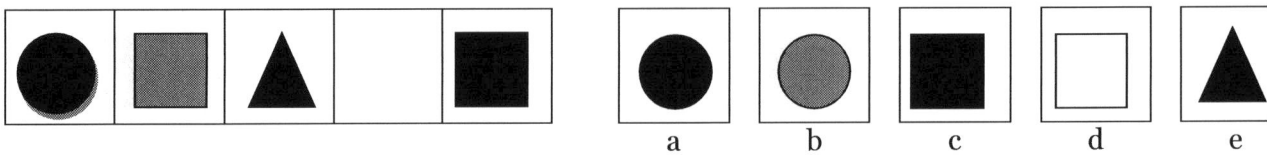

Answer: B

ii.

Which one of the shapes below is most different from the other four?

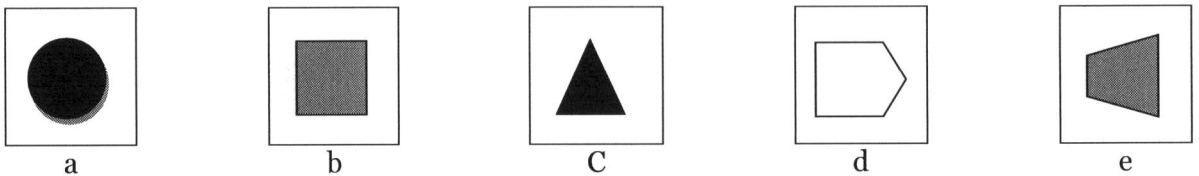

Answer: A

To the left of each line are five squares. Find which square on the right belongs in the empty square.

1.

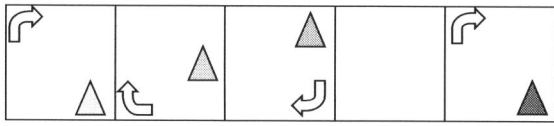 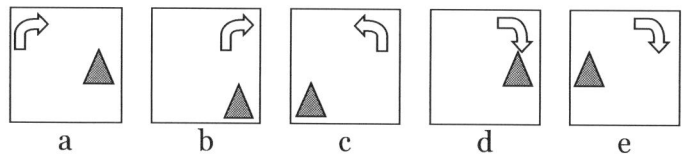

a   b   c   d   e

2.

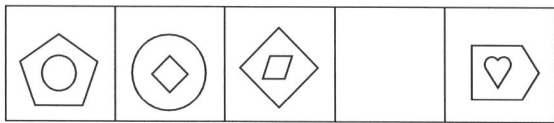 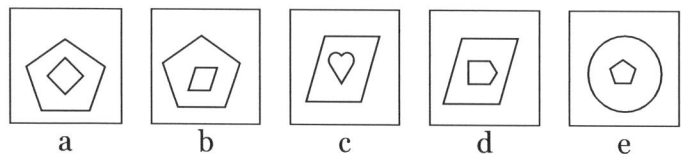

a   b   c   d   e

3.

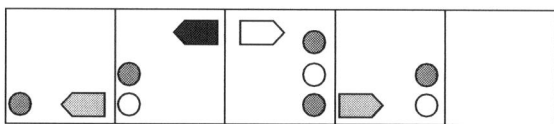 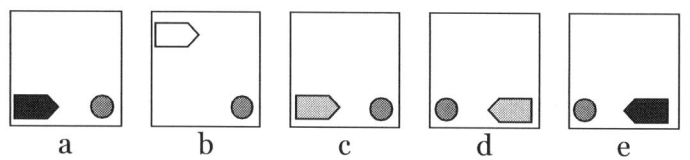

a   b   c   d   e

4.

 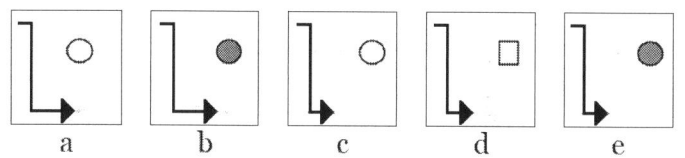

a   b   c   d   e

5.

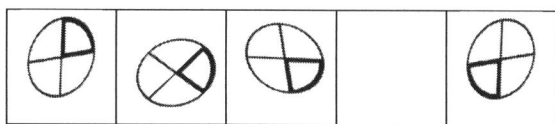 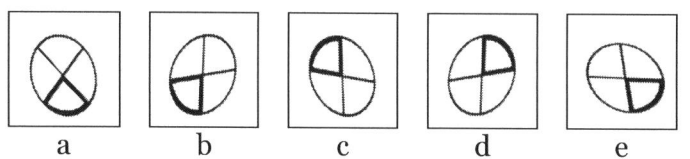

a   b   c   d   e

6.

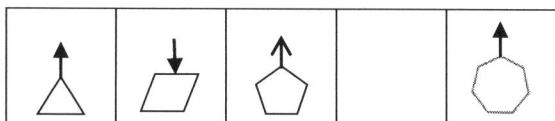 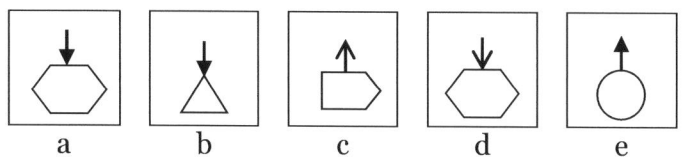

a   b   c   d   e

7.

a   b   c   d   e

8.

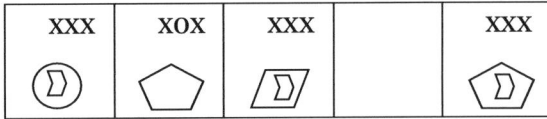

a   b   c   d   e

9.

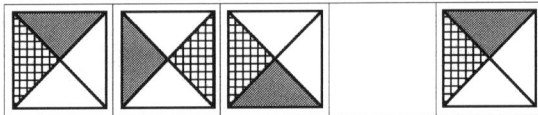

a   b   c   d   e

10.

a   b   c   d   e

Go on to the next page.

Which one of the shapes below is most different to the other four?

11.

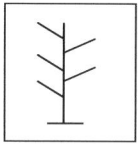   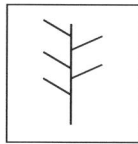      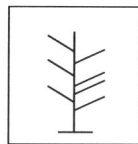   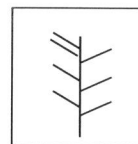

a   b   c   d   e

12.

a   b   c   d   e

13.

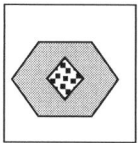   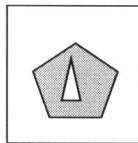         

a   b   c   d   e

14.

         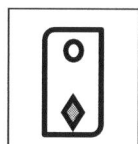   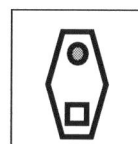

a   b   c   d   e

15.

   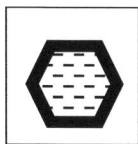   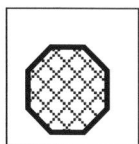      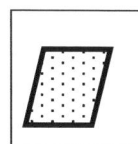

a   b   c   d   e

Go on to the next page.Go on to the next page.

16.

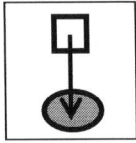
a

b

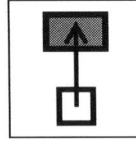
c

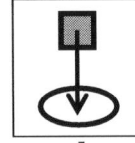
d

e

17.

a

b

c

d

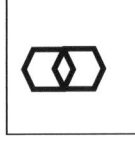
e

18.

a

b

c

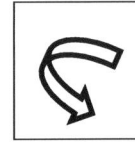
d

e

19.

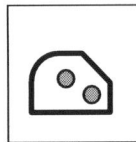
a

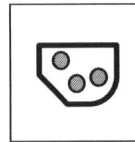
b

c

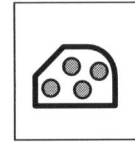
d

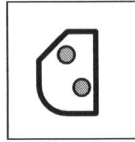
e

20.

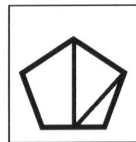
a

b

c

d

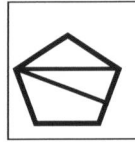
e

Do NOT go on to the next page until told to do so.

Examples

i. 12 x 3 =

ii. $\frac{3}{4} + \frac{1}{2} =$

A. 2

B. $\frac{2}{3}$

C. $1\frac{1}{4}$

D. $1\frac{3}{4}$

E. $\frac{1}{4}$

i.

0	3	6
[0]	[0]	[0]
[1]	[1]	[1]
[2]	[2]	[2]
[3]	[3]	[3]
[4]	[4]	[4]
[5]	[5]	[5]
[6]	[6]	[6]
[7]	[7]	[7]
[8]	[8]	[8]
[9]	[9]	[9]

ii. [A] [B] [C] [D] [E]

Do NOT go on until told to do so.

1.   171 sweets are shared equally between three brothers. How many does each brother get?

2.   Elvi left home at 7:36 and reached school at 8:07. How long did her journey take?

3.   In the triangle below each number is the sum of the two number directly underneath it.

```
                22
            8       14
          2   6       8
        1   1   5       3
```

What would be the top number for this triangle of numbers?

```
                ___
            ___     ___
        ___     8       5
      1     ___     ___     3
```

4.   Daniel travels 210 miles in 3 ½ hours. What is his average speed, in miles per hour?

5.   What is the missing number?

      _____ - 378 = 192

Go on to the next page.

6.   What is the missing number?

_____ + 3.78 = 5.19

7.   What is 30% of 600?

8.   Elliot buys 7 ice-creams at £1.20 each. How much will they cost?

9.   If Elliot has £20 how many ice-creams can he buy?

10.   3765 ÷ 15 =

11.   What is 28 x 34?

12.   In a class of 28, the ratio of girls to boys is 3:4. How many girls in the class?

13.   What is the highest common factor of 36 and 54?

Go on to the next page.

14. 95% of 80 children pass a Science test. How many do not pass?

15. Ella thinks of a number, adds eight then divides by seven. If the answer is 25, what was the original number?

16. Which is the largest number?
    a. 1.1
    b. 1.01
    c. 0.111
    d. 1.011
    e. 1.001

17. Take 567 away from 1200
    a. -633
    b. 632
    c. 633
    d. 732
    e. 733

18. Which is the smallest number?
    a. $\frac{1}{2}$
    b. $\frac{1}{10}$
    c. $\frac{3}{50}$
    d. $\frac{7}{65}$
    e. $\frac{1}{20}$

Go on to the next page.

19. What is 0.8 x 0.6 ?

    a. 0.0048

    b. 0.048

    c. 0.48

    d. 4.8

    e. 48

20. Put in the correct maths symbols in the expression below.

    322 ▢ 6 ▢ 3 = 644

    a. x, x

    b. x, ÷

    c. ÷, x

    d. ÷, +

    e. +, ÷

21. Convert 6.8 kg into grams.

    a. 68 000

    b. 6 800

    c. 6 008

    d. 680

    e. 608

22. If the temperature is 9°C and drops to -4°C at night, how much colder was the temperature at night?

    a. -13°C

    b. 5°C

    c. 5°C

    d. 13°C

    e. 14°C

Go on to the next page.

23. $1\frac{3}{4} + 2\frac{5}{6} =$

    a. $3\frac{4}{5}$

    b. $4\frac{4}{5}$

    c. $3\frac{7}{24}$

    d. $4\frac{7}{12}$

    e. $4\frac{9}{12}$

24. $1 \div 0.25 =$

    a. 0.0625

    b. 0.625

    c. 0.25

    d. 0.5

    e. 4

End of Test

11+

C.E.M. Style test

Set B: Paper 1

Read the following instructions carefully:

1. Do not open this booklet until told to do so.
2. You must answer the questions on the answer sheet provided.
3. You may do any rough working on a separate sheet of paper.
4. This test consists of four separately timed sections. You must not go on to the next section until you are told to do so.
5. Follow the instructions at the bottom of each page.
6. If you do make a mistake rub it out and put in your new answer.
7. Do not spend too long on a question, if a question is taking a long time move on to the next.
8. If you do not know the answer to the question, choose the answer you think best.
9. Not all sections have a time warning.
10. If you finish a section early you may go back and review any questions that are within the section that you are working on only. You must wait for further instructions before moving onto another section. You may not move back to a previous section.

Example

Read the passage below then answer the question that follows:

Spinach

Spinach is thought to be of Persian origin. By the tenth century it had spread across Europe. It gained popularity as the vegetable that gave, the cartoon character, Popeye his strength. However, it is the nutritional qualities and versatility that maintains its popularity today.

   i.   According to the above passage, which of the following is *not* true of spinach?
   - A.   It is a vegetable.
   - B.   It is very nutritious.
   - C.   It is eaten by Popeye.
   - D.   It comes from Europe.
   - E.   It is very popular.

The passage does not say that it comes from Europe but rather states that it is thought to have spread through Europe from Persia. Therefore the answer is D.

Do NOT go on to the next page.

Comprehension

Read the passage below then answer the questions that follow:

Chocolate

1 The chocolate industry is a big business in the UK, with annual sales of chocolate products
2 reaching an estimated £3.6 billion in recent years. However, while the sweet treat is clearly
3 in demand, not many people understand that there is more to a bar of chocolate than the
4 pristine foil wrapper and the divinely creamy taste.

5

6 Surprisingly, chocolate is actually derived from a plant, the *Theobroma cocao*, which is
7 more commonly known as the cocoa tree. The cocoa trees needed to produce chocolate
8 grow in countries with a very hot and rainy climate, this includes countries like Ghana,
9 Indonesia, Brazil, Peru and the Ivory Coast. Although cocoa is produced in many warmer
10 regions of the globe, most of the world's cocoa comes from western Africa. In fact, it is
11 estimated that about 43% of the world's chocolate is made from cocoa grown in the Ivory
12 Coast! The cocoa tree produces large cocoa pods which contain about fifty cocoa beans.
13 When the cocoa pods are ripe, harvesters go around the trees and pick off the pods by
14 hand to prevent damage to the pods. The beans can then be extracted from the pods and
15 fermented to form cocoa solids and cocoa butter, which are two of the main components
16 required to make chocolate. These products are then exported around the world to
17 countries like the United Kingdom where they can be processed and made into a variety of
18 chocolate commodities.

19

20 Whilst this process sounds simple, the demands on the cocoa farmers can be extreme as
21 cocoa farming is most common in regions where people are impoverished. Indeed, it is
22 not uncommon for regions of cocoa farming to have restricted access to clean running
23 water, healthcare and education. Moreover, due to the lack of the latter, many farmers are
24 exploited and are selling their cocoa products for extremely low prices. While the average
25 household in Britain spends £6.00 per week on chocolate, the average worker in a cocoa
26 plantation in Ghana or the Ivory Coast earns a little less than this. Cocoa farmers only
27 receiving 6% of the cost of the final chocolate product. Also, many cocoa plantations use
28 slavery and child labour. While most of the child labour is between the ages of 12 and 16,
29 children as young as five have been known to work on the farms. Further, ten percent of
30 child labourers in Ghana and 40% in the Ivory Coast do not attend school.

Go on to the next page.

31 However, Fairtrade Foundation schemes are helping to improve the conditions for cocoa
32 farmers and their communities, in particular throughout western Africa. The Fairtrade
33 Foundation is a charitable organisation that aims to improve conditions for farmers; it
34 ensures that farmers receive a fair price for their products and also helps to improve
35 facilities for the local people. They also ensure that the farms use neither slavery nor child
36 labour. Fairtrade schemes have been particularly instrumental in improving conditions
37 for cocoa farmers in recent years. Notably, in the Ivory Coast many villages supported by
38 The Fairtrade Foundation now have their own medical centres, schools and clean-water
39 pumps. These communities are supported by consumers in the UK choosing to purchase
40 chocolates branded with the Fairtrade mark, which guarantees that a fair price is being
41 paid for the cocoa and a premium is being paid to farming communities to improve
42 infrastructure.

43

44 Understanding the production of chocolate is important, however, it is also imperative to
45 consider the health effects associated with chocolate. Although chocolate is perceived as a
46 largely unhealthy snack, this is not wholly correct. Scientists have discovered that dark
47 chocolate can have many health benefits including lowering cholesterol levels and
48 reducing blood pressure. However, these effects only prove useful when dark chocolate is
49 consumed as part of a balanced diet. Moreover, the more popular milk chocolate contains
50 high quantities of fats and sugars which can lead to obesity, diabetes and other health
51 problems. Whilst chocolate may be a sweet enjoyed by the masses, it is important that
52 everyone remembers it is best consumed as a one off treat rather than an everyday
53 commodity.

1. What is the approximate total of annual chocolate sales in recent years?
    A. Around £4.
    B. Nearly £3 million.
    C. About £3.5 billion.
    D. More than £35 billion.
    E. £3.60.

2. If you wanted to make your own chocolate, what kind of plant would you need?
    A. A chocolate bush.
    B. Various types of hops.
    C. Two different types of trees.
    D. A cocoa tree.
    E. Chocolate seeds.

3. What is the annual income of an average cocoa farmer in the Ivory Coast?
    A. £6.00
    B. £5.67
    C. £10.00
    D. £300.
    E. £600.

4. Which of the following are not used in the process of making chocolate?
    A. Cocoa butter.
    B. Cocoa solids.
    C. Cocoa pod shells.
    D. None of the above are used making chocolate.
    E. All of the above are part of the chocolate-making process.

5. What is the most likely reason that cocoa trees are not grown in the UK?
    A. There is not enough room to grow the large trees.
    B. There are too many people on the land.
    C. People in the UK have enough money to have cocoa imported.
    D. The climate is too cold.
    E. Not enough people in the UK want cocoa trees.

6. What is one of the main purposes of the Fairtrade Foundation?
    A. To make sure that the amount of cocoa used in chocolate is even and fair.
    B. To ensure that in the UK, chocolate continues to be available at a low cost.
    C. To attempt to improve trade between the UK and Africa.
    D. To improve conditions for cocoa farmers.
    E. To make sure that cocoa farmers get lots of money for their cocoa.

7. Which of the following things has the Fairtrade Foundation not done?
    A. Paid a large amount of money for chocolate.
    B. Helped the Ivory Coast with medical centres.
    C. Helped the Ivory Coast with Schools.
    D. Helped the Ivory Coast with water pumps.
    E. Branded chocolates with the Fairtrade mark.

8. Most cocoa farmers live in areas that are
    A. In dire poverty.
    B. Cold and dry.
    C. Wealthy and prosperous.
    D. Near deserts.
    E. In Europe.

Go on to the next page.

9.   When it comes to health, chocolate:
      A.   Is always unhealthy.
      B.   Has no good health benefits.
      C.   Is a great snack to eat everyday.
      D.   Can reduce blood pressure to dangerous levels.
      E.   Has benefits when consumed as part of a balanced diet.

10.   Milk chocolate:
      A.   Is made from a different kind of cocoa tree.
      B.   Has high quantities of fat and sugars.
      C.   Lowers cholesterol levels.
      D.   Reduces blood pressure.
      E.   Has low quantities of fat and sugars.

11.   *Theobroma cocao* is
      A.   A brand of chocolate that is branded with the Fairtrade brand.
      B.   A small country in Africa that produces a great deal of cocoa.
      C.   Another name for a cocoa tree.
      D.   A by-product of the chocolate-making process.
      E.   The part of the cocoa tree that is not used to make chocolate.

12.   This article is most likely to be found in:
      A.   An encyclopaedia.
      B.   A dictionary.
      C.   A magazine.
      D.   A comic book.
      E.   A novel.

13.   Based on the reading, what is likely to be the writer's opinion of the Fairtrade
      Foundation?
      A.   The writer has no opinion.
      B.   The writer believes the Fairtrade Foundation is doing good work.
      C.   The writer believes the Fairtrade Foundation is doing poor work.
      D.   The writer believes the Fairtrade Foundation should stop the work they are
            doing.
      E.   The writer believes the Fairtrade Foundation is not actually fair.

14.   Why do harvesters of the cocoa pod pick the pods by hand?
      A.   Because they are too poor to afford machines.
      B.   Because it is too hot in the areas where cocoa trees grow.
      C.   To avoid damaging the beans in the pods.
      D.   Because climbing the trees is more fun than picking the pods off the ground.
      E.   To export the pods around the world.

Go on to the next page.

15. What is the main point of the third paragraph?
    A. Making chocolate is a long, involved process.
    B. Cocoa farmers are being exploited and live in poverty.
    C. Cocoa farming is a big business.
    D. The United Kingdom consumes a lot of chocolate.
    E. You can earn a lot of money farming cocoa.

16. How long do the pods of a cocoa tree take to ripen?
    A. 9 months.
    B. 6 days.
    C. 43 days.
    D. 2-3 months.
    E. The text does not provide this information.

17. Why should the reader understand the health effects of chocolate?
    A. Because that is the point of the entire text.
    B. Because chocolate does not deserve the negative image that it is given by health enthusiasts.
    C. Because the Fairtrade Foundation needs additional support.
    D. Because cocoa farmers are exploited.
    E. Because chocolate is a major commodity in the UK.

18. The making of cocoa solids is made difficult by:
    A. The heat.
    B. The lack of resources.
    C. The isolation of the cocoa farms.
    D. All of the above.
    E. None of the above.

19. The text says that the cocoa beans are "fermented." What does this mean?
    A. They are chilled and stored.
    B. They are packed tightly in boxes.
    C. They are placed in refrigerated rail cars.
    D. They sit, soften, and change their taste.
    E. They are stomped on by skilled workers.

20. Which of these is the closest in meaning to "exported?"
    A. Shipped.
    B. Mashed.
    C. Cooked.
    D. Eaten.
    E. Stored.

Go on to the next page.

21. When the text says that "farmers are being exploited," what does this mean?
    A. They are paid well.
    B. Being paid in water instead of money.
    C. Being used for their services.
    D. They are forced to hand-pick the pods from the cocoa trees.
    E. They do not have access to clean water.

22. The Fairtrade Foundation works to improve the infrastructure of the farming community. Which of these items would not be included in the infrastructure?
    A. Water pumps.
    B. Medical facilities.
    C. Roads.
    D. Mechanical pod-picking machines.
    E. Schools.

23. "Surprisingly, chocolate is actually derived from a plant ..." What type of word is "Surprisingly?"
    A. Noun.
    B. Adjective.
    C. Preposition.
    D. Verb.
    E. Adverb.

24. "The Cocoa tree produces large cocoa pods which contain about fifty cocoa beans." Which of these words is an adjective?
    A. Tree.
    B. Pods.
    C. Beans.
    D. Produces.
    E. Large.

25. What type of words are the following?

    Chocolate   **tree**   **products**   **farmers**

    A. Nouns.
    B. Adjectives.
    C. Prepositions.
    D. Verbs.
    E. Adverbs.

Do NOT go on to the next page.

Example

Choose the correct word, in the sentence below.

Big Ben

Big Ben is a well-known landmark on the London skyline. Big Ben is actually the name of the bell, while the tower is (nicknamed, officially, named, referred] known as the Elizabeth Tower.

Answer: officially

Cloze

Choose the correct word, in the passage below.

Thomas Edison and the Invention of the Lightbulb

Thomas Edison, was a famous inventor who held over one thousand [1](boxes, patents, warrants, charters) for different inventions. While he was a [2](plentiful, protea, prolific, careful) inventor, the lightbulb is the main invention in [3](everyday, use, clever, producing) today.

However, whether Edison invented the lightbulb or his [4](rival, competition, friendly, command) Swan is a matter of [5](conspiracy, contract, legal, debate). The story of the lightbulb starts in 1806 when Humphrey Davy produced a device called an arc lamp that he demonstrated to the Royal Society. The arc lamp produced light by creating an electric spark between two charcoal rods. However, it was [6](important, impenetrable, impractical, impersonal) for everyday use as it was too bright and used too much energy, so drained the batteries he used [7](slowly, quick, quickly, sparingly). However, when generators were invented the arc lamp was used by lighthouses and for other [8](impartial, industrial, frivolous, humorous) uses.

Scientists knew that when electricity passed through some [9](subspecies, substandard, substance, substances) they heated up and that if they became hot enough they would start to [10](bright, glow, glowing, fade). This was [11](showed, demonstrated, convinced, carried) by Volta as early as 1800. This was the principle behind the incandescent light bulb. The [12](problem, idea, creation, covenant) was that before long the material would [13](cringe, spark, burst, jump) into flame or melt. In 1841 a British scientist patented a bulb that used a vacuum to [14](help, infuse, test, stop) oxygen coming into contact with the hot substance and causing a fire. The bulb was [15](improvised, improved, improve, impoverished) by many scientists including Swan. Edison's system, demonstrated in 1879 was hailed as the first practical lightbulb.

In the question below, work out which net can be used to make the cube on the left.

Example:

 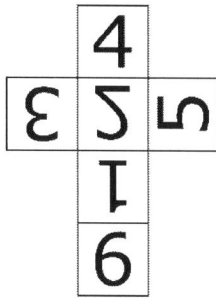 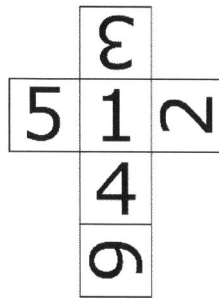 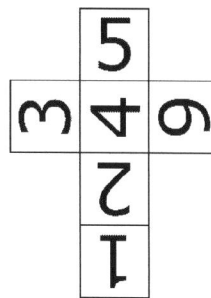 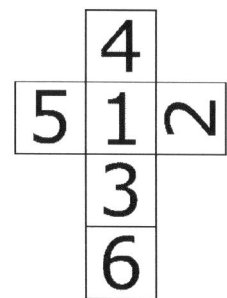

The answer is C.

In the questions below: Work out which net can be used to make the cube on the left.

1.

 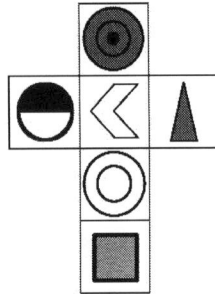 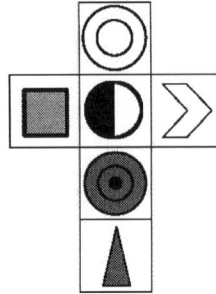 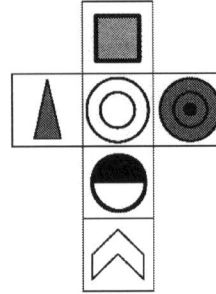 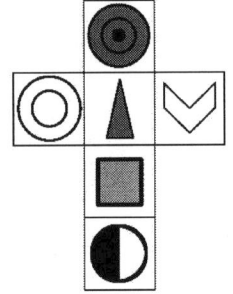

A.   B.   C.   D.

2.

  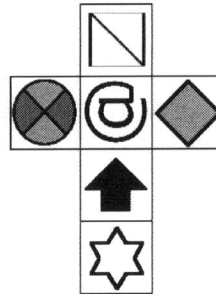 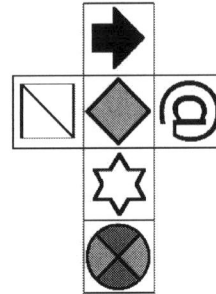 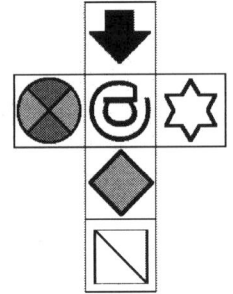

A.   B.   C.   D.

3.

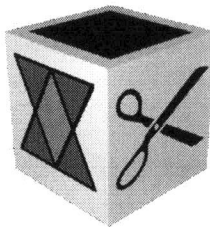    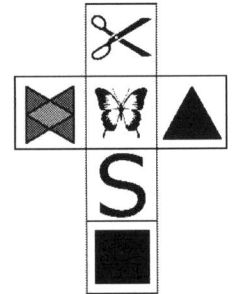

A.   B.   C.   D.

4.

 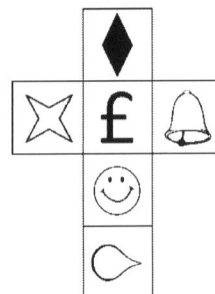 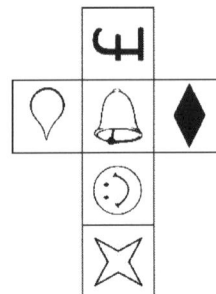 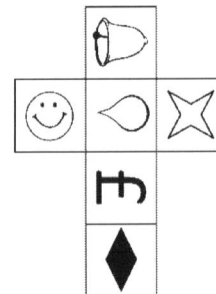 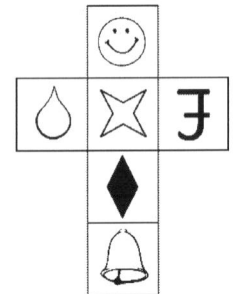

A.   B.   C.   D.

Go on to the next page.

5.

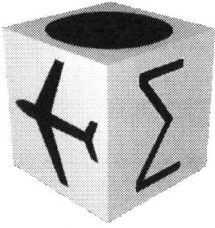 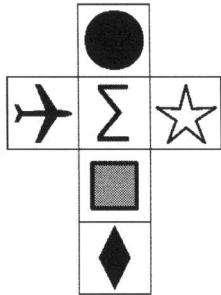 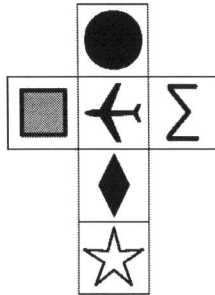 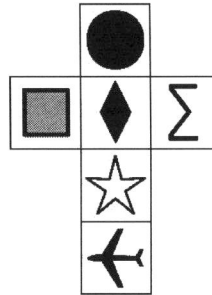 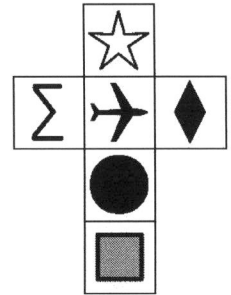

A.   B.   C.   D.

6.

 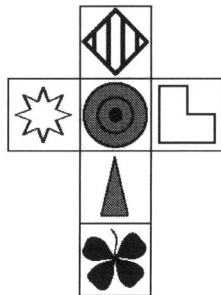 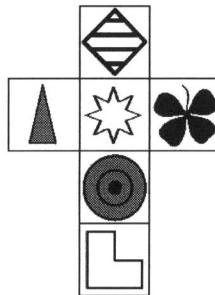 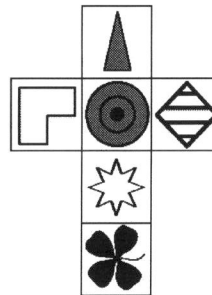 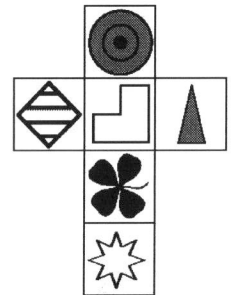

A.   B.   C.   D.

7.

 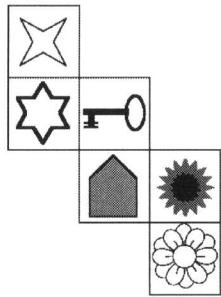 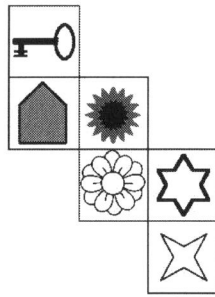 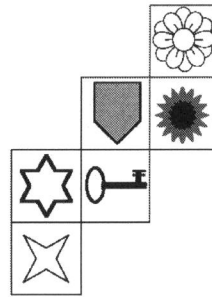 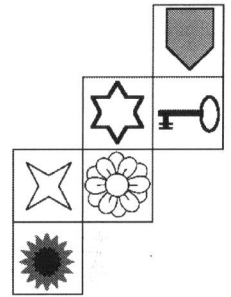

A.   B.   C.   D.

8.

 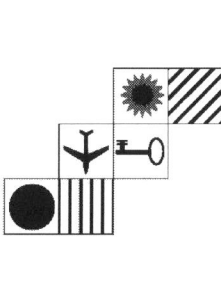   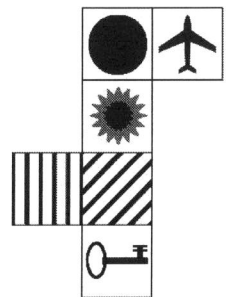

A.   B.   C.   D.

Go on to the next page.

9.

  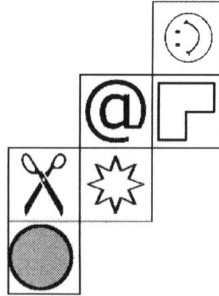 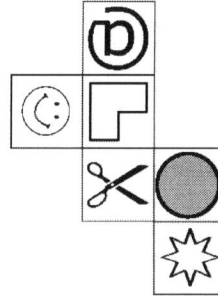 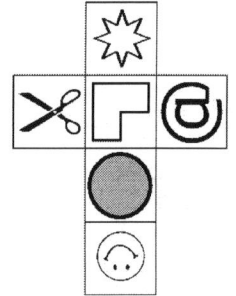

A.   B.   C.   D.

10.

 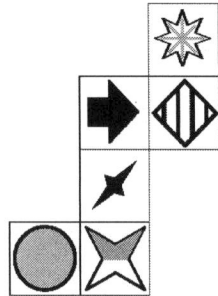 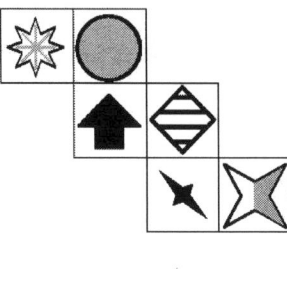 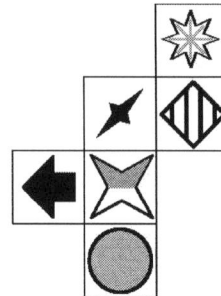 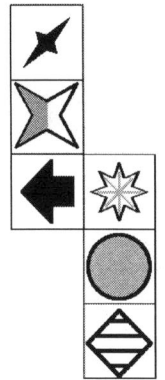

A.   B.   C.   D.

Example

i. Find the area of the rectangle below:

```
┌──────────────────────────────┐
│  20cm                        │
│                              │ 2.1cm
│                              │
└──────────────────────────────┘
```

Answer: 42 cm²

0	*4*	*2*
[0]	[0]	[0]
[1]	[1]	[1]
[2]	[2]	[2]
[3]	[3]	[3]
[4]	[4]	[4]
[5]	[5]	[5]
[6]	[6]	[6]
[7]	[7]	[7]
[8]	[8]	[8]
[9]	[9]	[9]

1. The sum of two numbers is 30. Their difference is six. What is the smallest number?

2. The series of patterns below are made from spotted and grey tiles. If the pattern is continued, what is the total number of tiles in pattern six?

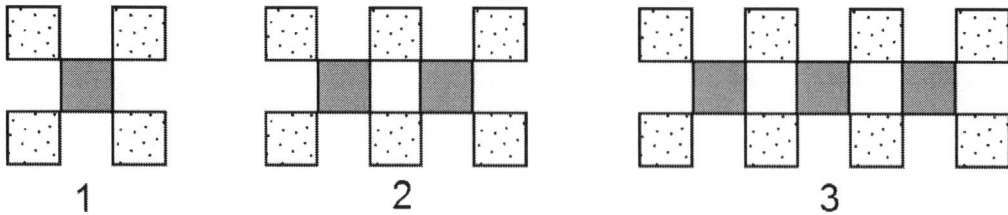

1   2   3

3. How many spotted squares are in pattern 45?

4. The area of the triangle below is 60cm^2.

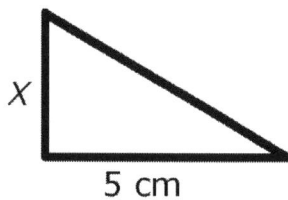

X

5 cm

Not drawn to scale.

What is the value of x in cm?

5. Amrit is landscaping his garden. He is using concrete slabs as shown below.

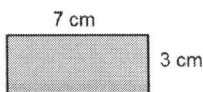

7 cm

3 cm

To make a garden bed, he put them in the following pattern.

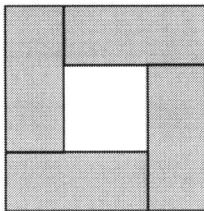

Not drawn to scale.

a. What is the area of the garden bed in the middle of the tiles in cm^2?

b. What area of the garden does the garden bed take up in cm^2?

Amrit then rearranges the tiles to make stepping stones like this.

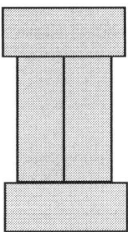

c. What is the outside perimeter of the stepping stones in cm?

Go on to the next page.

6. Ha and Tuan are friends. Ha gave a sixth of her stickers to Tuan. This increased Tuan's stickers from 10 to 15 stickers. How many stickers does Ha have now?

7. The table below shows the distance between eight cities, in miles.

Dartford							
20	London						
40	22	Slough					
69	45	28	Aylesbury				
90	60	43	26	Oxford			
142	118	110	186	79	Birmingham		
218	211	215	183	187	135	York	
276	269	274	240	245	193	77	Durham

a. If Cheng travels from Slough to York, how far does he travel, in miles? (assume he travels the shortest distance).

b. Cheng decides to visit his friend Richard on the way. Richard lives in Oxford. How much further will his journey be if he stops to visit Richard? (in miles)

c. If petrol costs £1.30 / litre and Cheng travelled an average of 10 miles / litre, how many litres would he use for his journey from Slough to York, visiting Richard on his way?

d. For part c above, how much would his petrol cost, to the nearest pound?

End of test.

11+

C.E.M. Style test

Set B: Paper 2

Read the following instructions carefully:

1. Do not open this booklet until told to do so.
2. You must answer the questions on the answer sheet provided.
3. You may do any rough working on a separate sheet of paper.
4. This test consists of five separately timed sections. You must not go on to the next section until you are told to do so.
5. Follow the instructions at the bottom of each page.
6. If you do make a mistake rub it out and put in your new answer.
7. Do not spend too long on a question, if a question is taking a long time move on to the next.
8. If you do not know the answer to the question, choose the answer you think best.
9. Not all sections have a time warning.
10. If you finish a section early you may go back and review any questions that are within the section that you are working on only. You must wait for further instructions before moving onto another section. You may not move back to a previous section.

This page has been deliberately left blank.

Example

Complete the words in the sentence below.

i. The w◯◯◯her has been very nice lately.

The word is weather, so the missing letters are E, A, T in that order.

e	a	t
[a]	[a̶]	[e]
[c]	[c]	[i]
[e̶]	[e]	[u]
[g]	[i]	[n]
[s]	[n]	[t̶]

Missing Letters

Complete the words in the passage below.

Stars

People have always been fascinated by the sky and our place in the universe. Many ancient ¹m☐☐☐s were based on the sky. Besides being used for religious ceremonies, stars were also used for navigation. Early astronomers arranged them in ²cons☐☐☐lations and used these to track the movement of the Sun and planets across the sky. The movement of these stars over a year ³ena☐☐☐d the first accurate calendars to be made, which were used to ⁴reg☐☐☐te agricultural practices. So the stars were very important to ⁵an☐☐☐nt civilisations.

We now know that stars are large spheres of gas and ⁶pl☐☐☐a, that are held together by their own gravity. For at least part of their life a star produces large quantities of heat and light due to the ⁷fu☐☐☐n of hydrogen. These ⁸r☐☐☐tions produce helium.

While many early astronomers thought the stars were unchanging, early Chinese astronomers knew that stars could appear. Stars start as clouds of gas called nebulas. They then live for billions of years before they die. How they die depends on the type of star. The larger stars are the most dramatic, forming a large ⁹explos☐☐☐ called a supernova. For a ¹⁰c☐☐☐le of weeks the supernova outshines the entire ¹¹gal☐☐☐ and ¹²rad☐☐☐es colossal amounts of energy. The core is ¹³squ☐☐☐ed by gravity into a neutron star or for the largest stars, where the energy is even more intense, a black hole is formed. Black holes are regions of space that are so dense with such a large gravity that even light cannot escape them. As a result, unlike stars which ¹⁴fl☐☐☐esce in a number of characteristic colours by which they are categorised, black holes emit no light at all.

Do NOT go on to the next page.

Example

Find the word which will go with both pairs of words.

i.   (glue, paste) (branch, twig)   adhesive, stick, adherent, bough
     Answer: stick

i. adhesive	[ ]
stick	[—]
adherent	[ ]
bough	[ ]

Do NOT go on to the next page.

Find the word which will go with both pairs of words.

1. (only, exclusive) (flatfish, cod)   alone, sole, mere, haddock, plaice

2. (mix, fold) (tease, annoy)   stir, add, churn, mock, rib

3. (hide, skin) (hurl, throw)   animal, leather, bombard, slam, pelt

4. (car, train) (chisel, hammer)   plane, boat, driver, tram, saw

5. (transport, carry) (monkey, dog)   move, hold, cat, wolf, bear

6. (cost, price) (attack, stampede)   demand, charge, levy, rush, storm

7. (assemble, patch) (rock, pave)   implement, construct, fabricate, stone, cobble

8. (button, zip) (fold, bow)   fastener, buckle, tie, crease, warp

9. (raisin, date) (trim, lop)   apricot, fig, prune, day, trip

10. (Summer, period) (herb, spice)   Autumn, Winter, era, season, chili

11. (basis, reason) (dirt, soil)   thought, footing, base, ground, earth

12. (exempt, relieve) (extra, additional)   free, absolve, reserve, surplus, spare

13. (answer, result) (salt water, mixture)   solution, method, composite, compound, tea

14. (pristine, new) (sage, thyme)   rosemary, basil, mint, parsley, yarrow

15. (lump, heap) (crowd, multitude)   pile, mass, bulk, clump, cloud

16. (cast, moult) (hut, shack)   shed, barn, hovel, discard, doff

17. (paperclip, fastener) (essential, main)   fundamental, standard, chief, pivotal, staple

18. (speak, talk) (total, complete)   utter, say, voice, absolute, unequivocal

19. (search, scour) (brush, disentangle)   groom, neaten, comb, tease, rake

20. (thing, gadget) (disagree, oppose)   item, object, device, entity, condemn

Example

Find the word which is the most similar in meaning to the word on the left.

i.   come   near, go, depart, arrive

i. near	[ ]
go	[ ]
depart	[ ]
arrive	[H]

Do NOT go on to the next page.

Which word is the most similar in meaning to the word on the left.

1. edify — enlighten, change, improve, correct

2. justify — fair, rationalise, correct, excuse

3. start — instigate, conclude, indicative, initiate

4. banquet — eat, table, feast, famine

5. contaminate — river, ocean, dirt, pollute

6. refuse — throw, negative, decline, unable

7. idiotic — ludicrous, atrocious, stamina, germinate

8. promising — daring, laughing, pleasing, hopeful

9. abrasive — adhesive, harsh, comment, strong

10. lucid — clever, coherent, fatuous, fatuitous

11. superb — nice, solar, brilliant, light

12. astute — courage, strength, shrewd, startling

13. clear — simple, translucent, transparent, opaque

14. empty — vacate, airtight, tenant, haunted

15. help — find, ailing, assist, wrought

16. blossom — flour, flourish, garnish, plume

17. frantic — fear, crazy, temperate, distraught

18. discretion — judgement, inattention, omission, concern

19. adverse — caesura, allusion, append, unfavourable

20. obstinate — infant, yielding, adamant, blemish

Do NOT go on to the next page.

Examples

In the grid below, one square has been left empty. Choose the answer that should fill the empty square.

i.

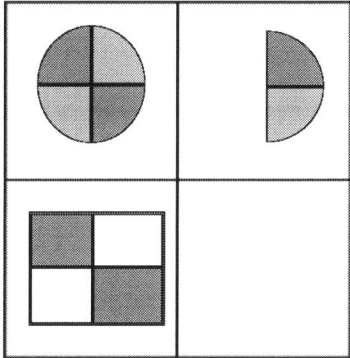
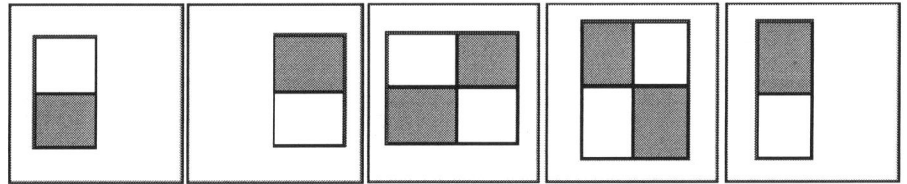

Answer: B.

In the squares below, choose the square that is different to the other three.

ii.

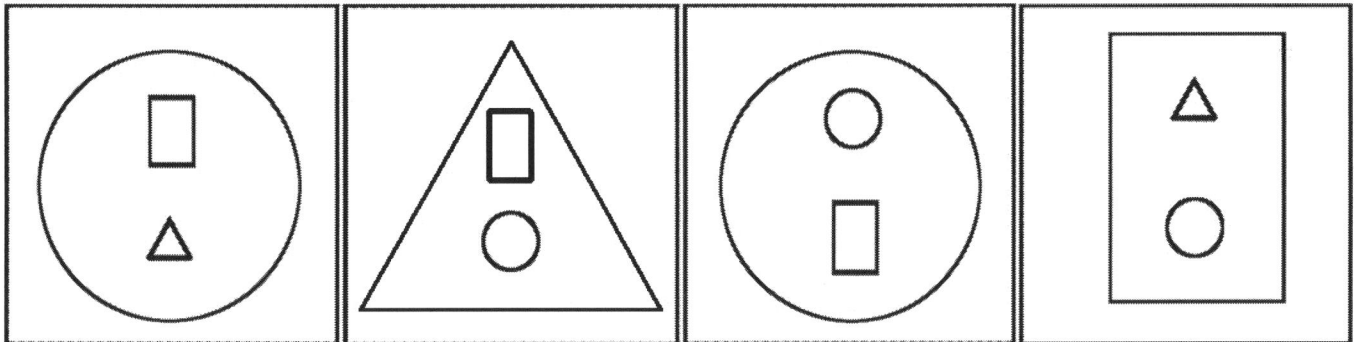

Answer: C.

Do NOT go on to the next page.

In the grids below, one square has been left empty. Choose the answer that should fill the empty square.

1.

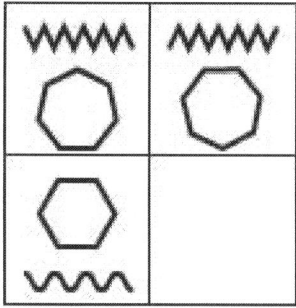
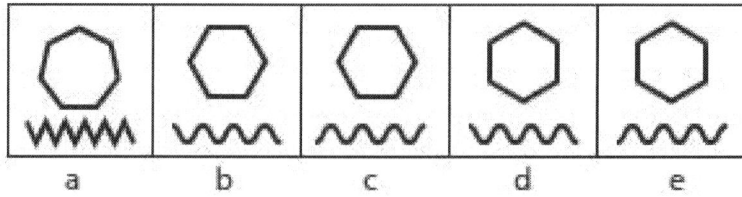

a   b   c   d   e

2.

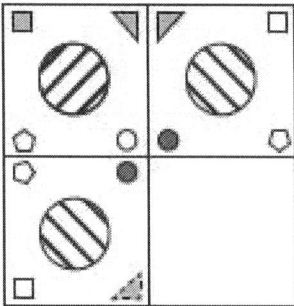
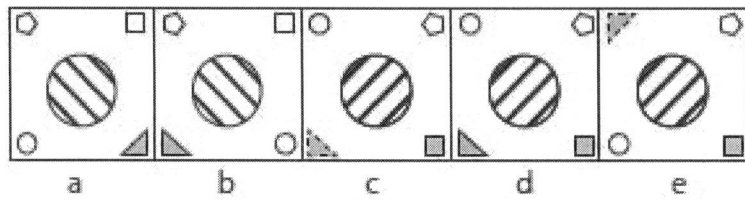

a   b   c   d   e

3.

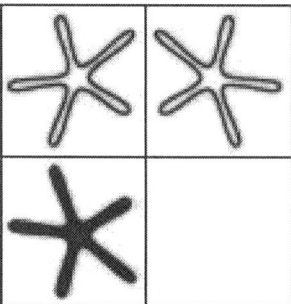
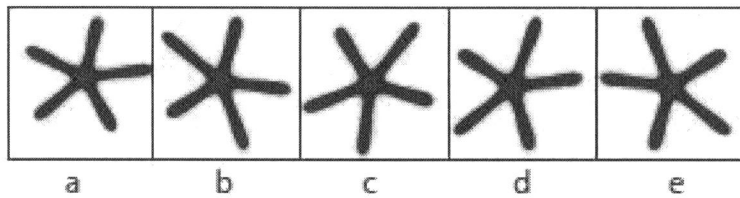

a   b   c   d   e

4.

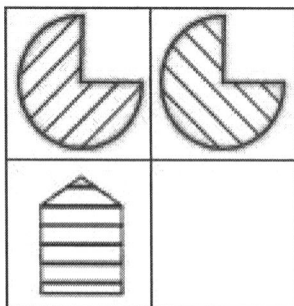
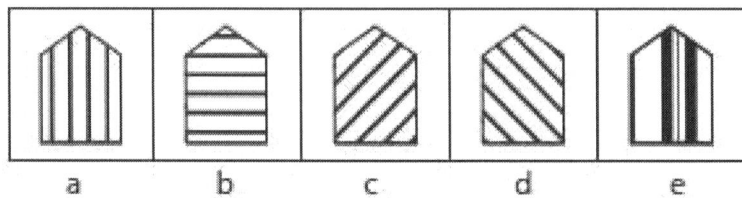

a   b   c   d   e

5

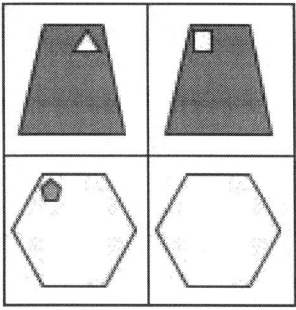 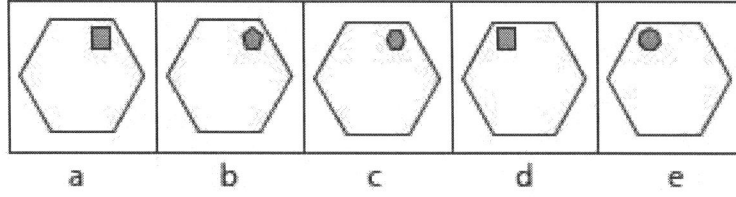

6.

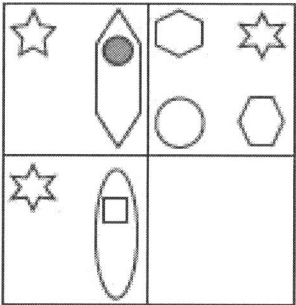 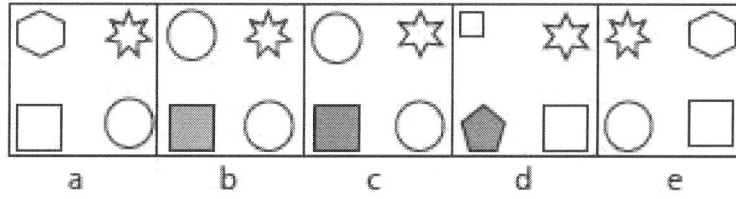

7.

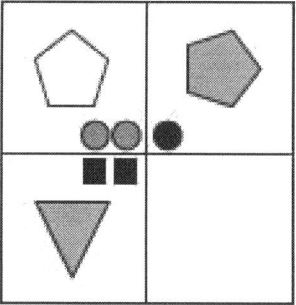 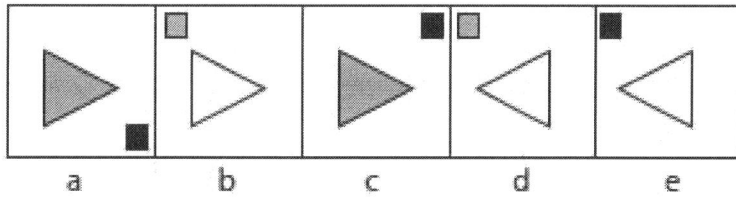

8.

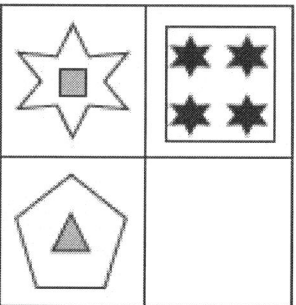 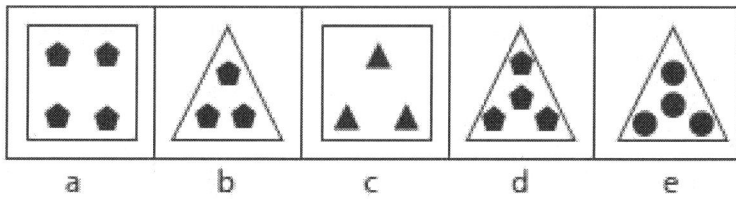

Go on to the next page.

9

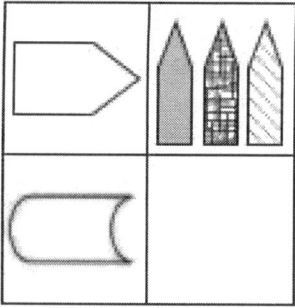

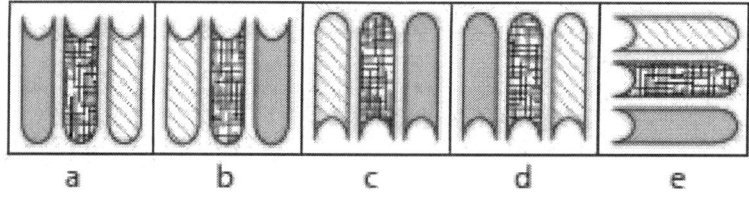

10.

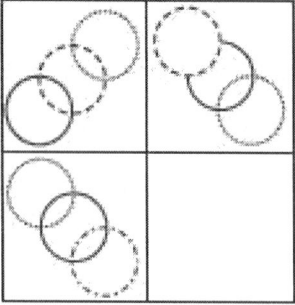

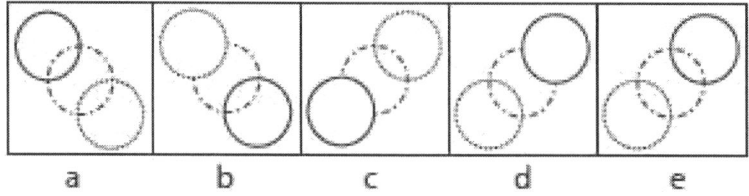

In the squares below, choose the square that is different to the other three.

11

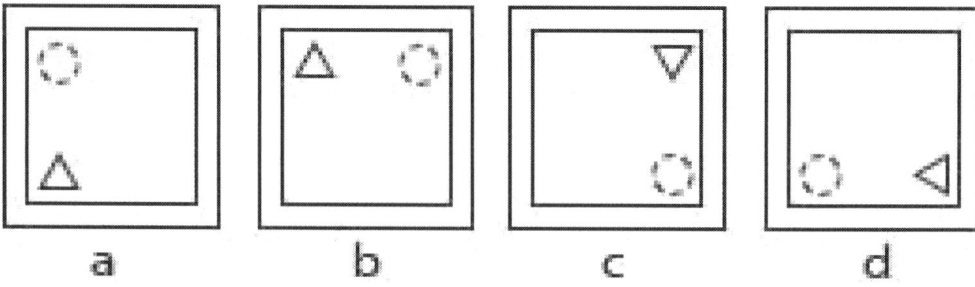

12.

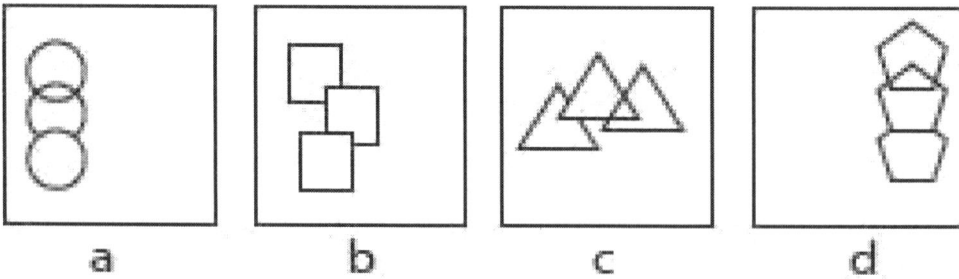

Go on to the next page.

13.

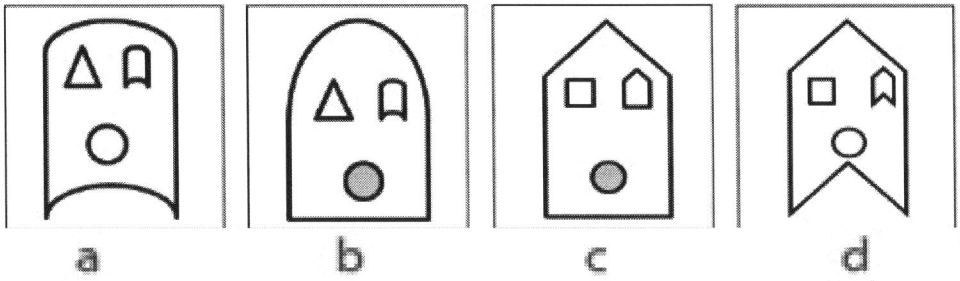

a   b   c   d

14.

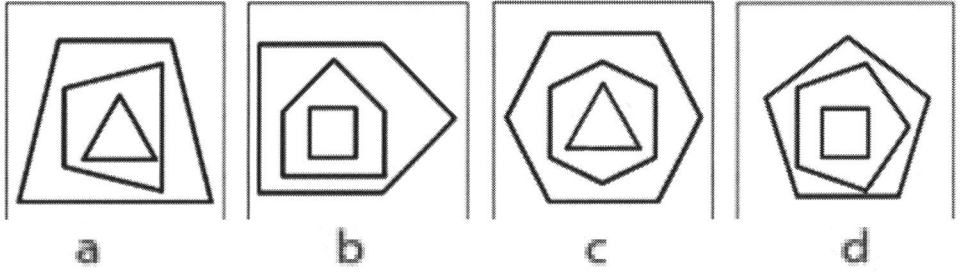

a   b   c   d

15.

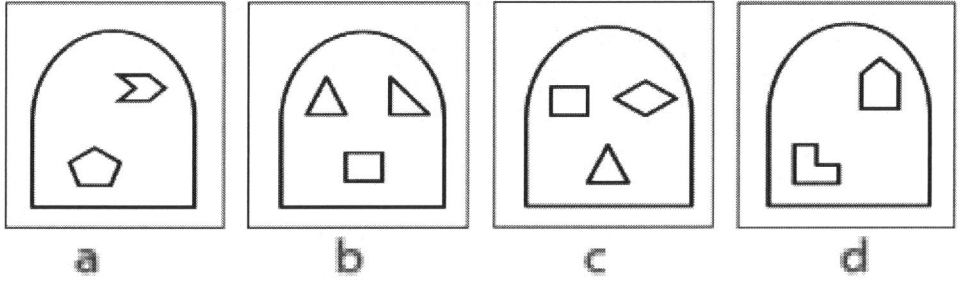

a   b   c   d

16.

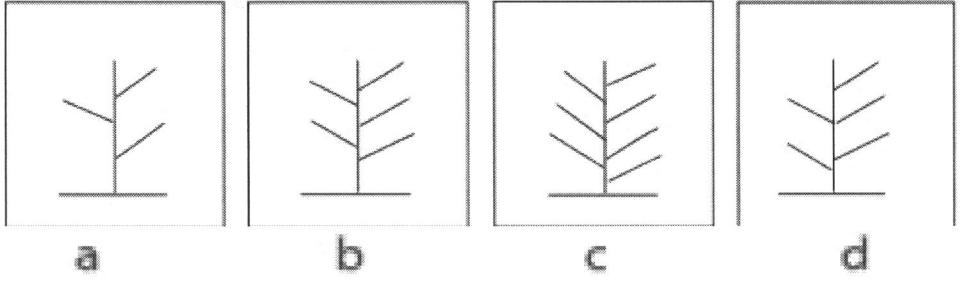

a   b   c   d

17.

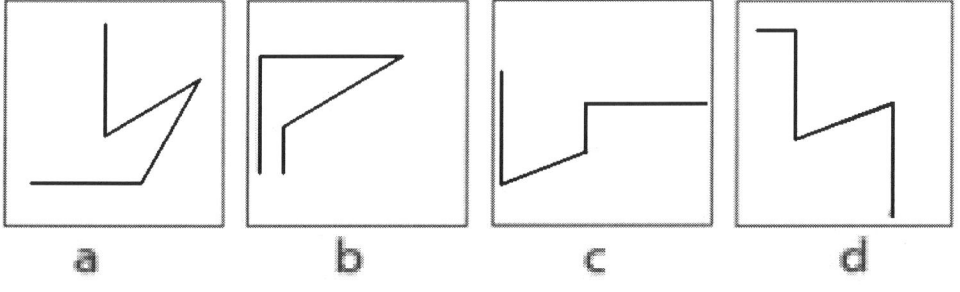

a   b   c   d

Go on to the next page.

18.

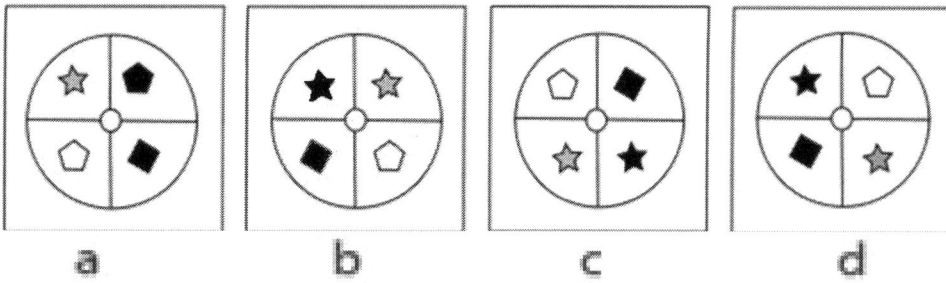

a   b   c   d

19.

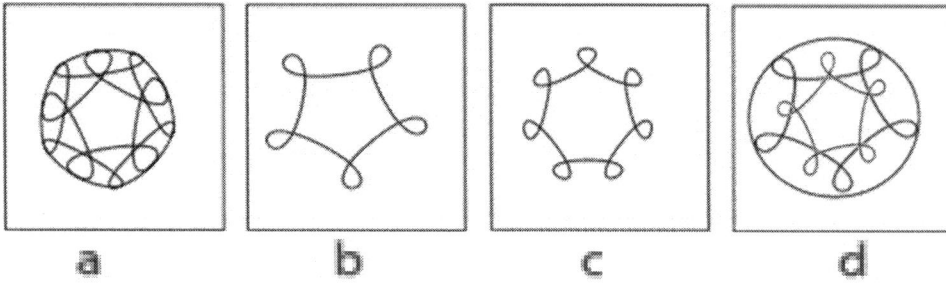

a   b   c   d

20.

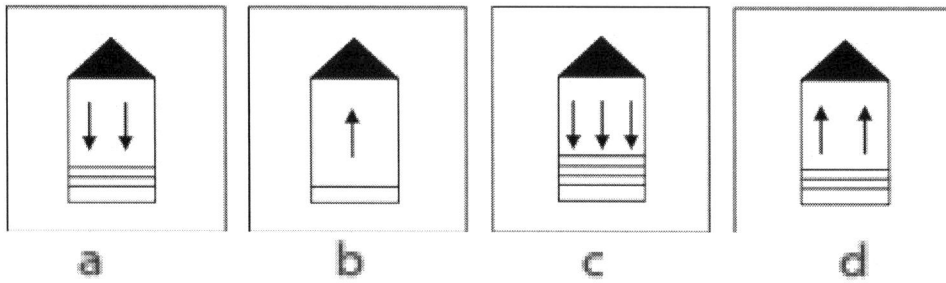

a   b   c   d

Do NOT go on to the next page.

Examples

i. 441 ÷ 7 =

ii. 50% of $\frac{1}{2}$ =

A. 2

B. $\frac{1}{10}$

C. $\frac{1}{100}$

D. $\frac{1}{4}$

E. 1

i.

ii. [A] [B] [C] [D] [E]

0	6	3
[0]	[0]	[0]
[1]	[1]	[1]
[2]	[2]	[2]
[3]	[3]	[3]
[4]	[4]	[4]
[5]	[5]	[5]
[6]	[6]	[6]
[7]	[7]	[7]
[8]	[8]	[8]
[9]	[9]	[9]

Do NOT go on to the next page.

1. $3\frac{2}{5} - 2\frac{3}{7} =$

   A. $1\frac{1}{12}$

   B. $1\frac{1}{35}$

   C. $5\frac{29}{35}$

   D. $\frac{34}{35}$

   E. $5\frac{5}{12}$

2. $\frac{n}{4} = 36$ What is the value of n?

   A. 6

   B. 9

   C. 12

   D. 18

   E. 144

3. Complete the sequence:

   3, -6, 18, -72

   A. -360

   B. -126

   C. 84

   D. 126

   E. 360

4. -7 + 11 =

   A. -18

   B. -4

   C. 4

   D. 11

   E. 77

5. Felicity was 11 years and 5 months old in March 2014. In what month and year was she born?

   A. August 2002

   B. August 2003

   C. August 2004

   D. November 2002

   E. November 2003

Go on to the next page.Go on to the next page.Go on to the next page.

6.   Jeb went shopping. 1 kg of flour cost 85p. How much is 600g worth?
      A. 17p
      B. 41p
      C. 51p
      D. 71p
      E. £1.42

7.   What is the missing number in this table?

4	10	16	18	26
3	6	9	10	

8.   65 x 49 =

9. $25\overline{)3789}$ to the nearest whole number

10.   A map has a scale of 1:900 000. On the map two bridges along a river are only
      3mm apart. How many kilometres apart are the bridges?

11.   There are five chess players. Each player plays every other player once. How
      many chess games are played?

12.   Mrs Sharma goes to the shop. She spends £11.80. However, she has a 35% off
      voucher for the opening sale. How much does she save?

13.   Four teenagers go on a shopping spree. Three of the teenagers spend an average
      of £6. All four teenagers spend an average of £7. How much did the fourth
      teenager spend?

14.   Tarryn's watch loses six minutes every day. How many seconds does it lose an
      hour?

Go on to the next page.

Art and Craft Shop

Open: 8:00 a.m.

Closed for lunch: 12:30 – 1:15 p.m.

Closed: 4:30 p.m.

15. How long is the shop open each day? (give your answer in hours as a decimal)

16. Satvia started with £15. She saved the same amount every week from her pocket money. After twelve weeks she had saved £87. How much had she saved after seven weeks?

17. The shape below is a regular hexagon. What is its area?

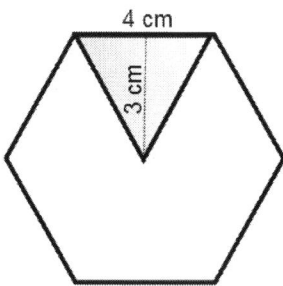

4 cm

3 cm

18. Look at the following patterns made by matchsticks.

1   2   3

How many matchsticks would be in the fifteenth pattern?

19. Sian buys a pack of eight ice-creams for £5 and sells them for £1 each. What percentage profit does she make?

20. Riya and Guneer have parcels. Riya's parcel is 6 kg heavier. If both parcels together have a mass of 28 kg, how heavy is Guneer's parcel?

End of test.

Instructions:

1. Check that you are marking the answer for the correct question number.
2. Mark ONE answer only for each question.
3. Mark boxes like this: [A]
4. Use an HB pencil and rub out any errors thoroughly.

Comprehension

Example

i. [A] [B] [C] [D]

Questions

1. [A] [B] [C] [D]
2. [A] [B] [C] [D]
3. [A] [B] [C] [D]
4. [A] [B] [C] [D]
5. [A] [B] [C] [D]
6. [A] [B] [C] [D]
7. [A] [B] [C] [D]
8. [A] [B] [C] [D]

Non-Verbal Ability

Example

i. [A] [B] [C] [D]

Questions

1. [A] [B] [C] [D]
2. [A] [B] [C] [D]
3. [A] [B] [C] [D]
4. [A] [B] [C] [D]
5. [A] [B] [C] [D] [E] [F]
6. [A] [B] [C] [D] [E] [F]
7. [A] [B] [C] [D] [E] [F]

Verbal Activity

Example

i.

c	e	i
[a]	[a]	[e]
[c]	[c]	[i]
[e]	[e]	[u]
[g]	[i]	[n]
[s]	[n]	[t]

ii. uncle   [   ]
    grandfather   [   ]
    niece   [   ]
    nephew   [   ]

Questions

1.

[a]	[a]	[a]
[e]	[c]	[e]
[o]	[e]	[o]
[r]	[r]	[n]
[s]	[t]	[t]

2.

[a]	[a]	[e]
[c]	[c]	[i]
[d]	[e]	[u]
[e]	[i]	[n]
[h]	[s]	[s]

3.

[a]	[a]	[a]	[a]
[c]	[c]	[e]	[e]
[e]	[d]	[i]	[i]
[i]	[i]	[u]	[l]
[s]	[n]	[t]	[u]

4.

[c]	[a]	[a]
[d]	[c]	[b]
[g]	[e]	[d]
[p]	[i]	[i]
[s]	[s]	[v]

5.

[e]	[a]	[e]
[h]	[c]	[i]
[i]	[e]	[o]
[o]	[i]	[u]
[r]	[o]	[y]

6.

[a]	[a]	[a]
[c]	[c]	[e]
[s]	[e]	[i]
[t]	[n]	[o]
[u]	[m]	[u]

7. Spain   [   ]
   France   [   ]
   Hungary   [   ]
   Japan   [   ]

8. potato   [   ]
   apple   [   ]
   grape   [   ]
   mango   [   ]

9. whale   [   ]
   manatee   [   ]
   gecko   [   ]
   meerkat   [   ]

10. train   [   ]
    car   [   ]
    plain   [   ]
    ship   [   ]

11. filthy   [   ]
    stingy   [   ]
    dirty   [   ]
    grimy   [   ]

12. reduce   [   ]
    demolish   [   ]
    diminish   [   ]
    decrease   [   ]

13. pledge   [   ]
    prize   [   ]
    award   [   ]
    trophy   [   ]

14. strict   [   ]
    stern   [   ]
    husky   [   ]
    stringent   [   ]

15. tune   [   ]
    anthem   [   ]
    composer   [   ]
    hymn   [   ]

16. listen   [   ]
    tinsel   [   ]
    silent   [   ]
    hear   [   ]

Cubes
Example
i. [A] [B] [~~C~~] [D]

Questions
1. [A] [B] [C] [D]
2. [A] [B] [C] [D]
3. [A] [B] [C] [D]
4. [A] [B] [C] [D]
5. [A] [B] [C] [D]
6. [A] [B] [C] [D]
7. [A] [B] [C] [D]
8. [A] [B] [C] [D]
9. [A] [B] [C] [D]
10. [A] [B] [C] [D]

Numerical Reasoning
Examples

i.

0	4	2	cm²
[~~0~~]	[0]	[0]	
[1]	[1]	[1]	
[2]	[2]	[~~2~~]	
[3]	[3]	[3]	
[4]	[~~4~~]	[4]	
[5]	[5]	[5]	
[6]	[6]	[6]	
[7]	[7]	[7]	
[8]	[8]	[8]	
[9]	[9]	[9]	

ii.

7	.	7	cm
[0]	.	[0]	
[1]	.	[1]	
[2]	.	[2]	
[3]	.	[3]	
[4]	.	[4]	
[5]	.	[5]	
[6]	.	[6]	
[~~7~~]	.	[~~7~~]	
[8]	.	[8]	
[9]	.	[9]	

Numerical Reasoning
Questions

1.

[0]	[0]	[0]
[1]	[1]	[1]
[2]	[2]	[2]
[3]	[3]	[3]
[4]	[4]	[4]
[5]	[5]	[5]
[6]	[6]	[6]
[7]	[7]	[7]
[8]	[8]	[8]
[9]	[9]	[9]

2.

[0]	[0]	[0]
[1]	[1]	[1]
[2]	[2]	[2]
[3]	[3]	[3]
[4]	[4]	[4]
[5]	[5]	[5]
[6]	[6]	[6]
[7]	[7]	[7]
[8]	[8]	[8]
[9]	[9]	[9]

3.

[0]	[0]	[0]
[1]	[1]	[1]
[2]	[2]	[2]
[3]	[3]	[3]
[4]	[4]	[4]
[5]	[5]	[5]
[6]	[6]	[6]
[7]	[7]	[7]
[8]	[8]	[8]
[9]	[9]	[9]

4.

	.		
[0]	.	[0]	[0]
[1]	.	[1]	[1]
[2]	.	[2]	[2]
[3]	.	[3]	[3]
[4]	.	[4]	[4]
[5]	.	[5]	[5]
[6]	.	[6]	[6]
[7]	.	[7]	[7]
[8]	.	[8]	[8]
[9]	.	[9]	[9]

5. min

[0]	[0]
[1]	[1]
[2]	[2]
[3]	[3]
[4]	[4]
[5]	[5]
[6]	[6]
[7]	[7]
[8]	[8]
[9]	[9]

6.

	:		
[0]	:	[0]	[0]
[1]	:	[1]	[1]
[2]	:	[2]	[2]
[3]	:	[3]	[3]
[4]	:	[4]	[4]
[5]	:	[5]	[5]
[6]	:	[6]	[6]
[7]	:	[7]	[7]
[8]	:	[8]	[8]
[9]	:	[9]	[9]

7.

[0]	[0]	[0]
[1]	[1]	[1]
[2]	[2]	[2]
[3]	[3]	[3]
[4]	[4]	[4]
[5]	[5]	[5]
[6]	[6]	[6]
[7]	[7]	[7]
[8]	[8]	[8]
[9]	[9]	[9]

8.

[0]	[0]	[0]
[1]	[1]	[1]
[2]	[2]	[2]
[3]	[3]	[3]
[4]	[4]	[4]
[5]	[5]	[5]
[6]	[6]	[6]
[7]	[7]	[7]
[8]	[8]	[8]
[9]	[9]	[9]

9. g

[0]	[0]
[1]	[1]
[2]	[2]
[3]	[3]
[4]	[4]
[5]	[5]
[6]	[6]
[7]	[7]
[8]	[8]
[9]	[9]

10.

[0]	[0]	[0]
[1]	[1]	[1]
[2]	[2]	[2]
[3]	[3]	[3]
[4]	[4]	[4]
[5]	[5]	[5]
[6]	[6]	[6]
[7]	[7]	[7]
[8]	[8]	[8]
[9]	[9]	[9]

11. cm²

[0]	[0]
[1]	[1]
[2]	[2]
[3]	[3]
[4]	[4]
[5]	[5]
[6]	[6]
[7]	[7]
[8]	[8]
[9]	[9]

12. £

	.		
[0]	.	[0]	[0]
[1]	.	[1]	[1]
[2]	.	[2]	[2]
[3]	.	[3]	[3]
[4]	.	[4]	[4]
[5]	.	[5]	[5]
[6]	.	[6]	[6]
[7]	.	[7]	[7]
[8]	.	[8]	[8]
[9]	.	[9]	[9]

Set A Paper 2

Instructions:

1. Check that you are marking the answer for the correct question number.
2. Mark ONE answer only for each question.
3. Mark boxes like this: [~~A~~]
4. Use an HB pencil and rub out any errors thoroughly.

Comprehension

Example

i. [A] [B] [C] [~~D~~] [E]

Question

1. [A] [B] [C] [D] [E]
2. [A] [B] [C] [D] [E]
3. [A] [B] [C] [D] [E]
4. [A] [B] [C] [D] [E]
5. [A] [B] [C] [D] [E]
6. [A] [B] [C] [D] [E]
7. [A] [B] [C] [D] [E]

Verbal Activity

Example

i.

e	o	w
[a]	[a]	[e]
[c]	[c]	[i-]
[~~e~~]	[~~o~~]	[u]
[g]	[i]	[n]
[s]	[n]	[~~w~~]

ii. flat   [   ]
   start   [   ]
   end   [~~ ~~]
   because   [   ]

Question

1.

[a]	[a]	[e]
[e]	[e]	[d]
[i]	[i]	[m]
[o]	[o]	[n]
[u]	[u]	[t]

Verbal Activity Continued

2.

[a]	[a]	[e]
[c]	[c]	[i]
[e]	[e]	[n]
[h]	[i]	[u]
[s]	[s]	[s]

3.

[a]	[a]	[a]	[a]
[e]	[c]	[n]	[c]
[i]	[d]	[r]	[i]
[o]	[i]	[u]	[l]
[s]	[n]	[t]	[s]

4.

[a]	[a]	[a]
[c]	[c]	[d]
[h]	[e]	[e]
[l]	[l]	[l]
[o]	[n]	[n]

5.

[e]	[a]	[e]
[f]	[c]	[i]
[g]	[l]	[h]
[h]	[s]	[s]
[m]	[t]	[y]

6.

[p]	[a]	[a]
[r]	[c]	[e]
[s]	[e]	[i]
[t]	[n]	[o]
[w]	[s]	[u]

7.

[c]	[a]	[a]
[d]	[e]	[d]
[f]	[f]	[e]
[m]	[i]	[l]
[n]	[r]	[n]

8.

[b]	[a]	[a]
[c]	[c]	[d]
[d]	[l]	[e]
[h]	[m]	[s]
[s]	[n]	[y]

9.

[a]	[a]	[a]
[h]	[c]	[e]
[i]	[e]	[i]
[t]	[n]	[o]
[u]	[m]	[u]

10.

[a]	[a]	[a]
[e]	[c]	[e]
[h]	[m]	[i]
[i]	[o]	[r]
[r]	[r]	[t]

11.

[a]	[a]	[c]
[e]	[c]	[i]
[i]	[l]	[h]
[o]	[s	[s]
[u]	[t]	[y]

12.

[a]	[a]	[m]
[c]	[c]	[n]
[s]	[e]	[r]
[t]	[n]	[s]
[u]	[r]	[y]

13.

[f]	[a]	[a]
[g]	[e]	[b]
[h]	[i]	[d]
[m]	[o]	[o]
[r]	[u]	[u]

14.

[a]	[a]	[l]
[c]	[e]	[n]
[s]	[i]	[p]
[t]	[o]	[r]
[w]	[u]	[s]

15.	is	[ ]	23.	treat	[ ]
	practice	[ ]		treated	[ ]
	day	[ ]		like	[ ]
	good	[ ]		likes	[ ]
	the	[ ]		as	[ ]
16.	hurts	[ ]	24.	the	[ ]
	to	[ ]		it	[ ]
	throat	[ ]		around	[ ]
	sore	[ ]		once	[ ]
	my	[ ]		the	[ ]
17.	brush	[ ]	25.	he	[ ]
	teeth	[ ]		long	[ ]
	twice	[ ]		the	[ ]
	your	[ ]		was	[ ]
	times	[ ]		and	[ ]
18.	forecast	[ ]	26.	so	[ ]
	the	[ ]		it	[ ]
	weather	[ ]		a	[ ]
	day	[ ]		walk	[ ]
	said	[ ]		holidays	[ ]
19.	the	[ ]	27.	for	[ ]
	capital	[ ]		at	[ ]
	of	[ ]		went	[ ]
	is	[ ]		checkouts	[ ]
	was	[ ]		part-time	[ ]
20.	caused	[ ]	28.	day	[ ]
	not	[ ]		diary	[ ]
	late	[ ]		many	[ ]
	to	[ ]		keep	[ ]
	well	[ ]		a	[ ]
21.	stood	[ ]	29.	snowed	[ ]
	timetable	[ ]		hazardous	[ ]
	for	[ ]		night	[ ]
	people	[ ]		causing	[ ]
	the	[ ]		driving	[ ]
22.	on	[ ]	30.	before	[ ]
	sorting	[ ]		buy	[ ]
	is	[ ]		the	[ ]
	groups	[ ]		to	[ ]
	into	[ ]		time	[ ]

Non-Verbal Reasoning
Example
 i. [A] [B] [C] [D] [E]
 ii. [A] [B] [C] [D] [E]

Question
 1. [A] [B] [C] [D] [E]
 2. [A] [B] [C] [D] [E]
 3. [A] [B] [C] [D] [E]
 4. [A] [B] [C] [D] [E]
 5. [A] [B] [C] [D] [E]
 6. [A] [B] [C] [D] [E]
 7. [A] [B] [C] [D] [E]
 8. [A] [B] [C] [D] [E]
 9. [A] [B] [C] [D] [E]
10. [A] [B] [C] [D] [E]
11. [A] [B] [C] [D] [E]
12. [A] [B] [C] [D] [E]
13. [A] [B] [C] [D] [E]
14. [A] [B] [C] [D] [E]
15. [A] [B] [C] [D] [E]
16. [A] [B] [C] [D] [E]
17. [A] [B] [C] [D] [E]
18. [A] [B] [C] [D] [E]
19. [A] [B] [C] [D] [E]
20. [A] [B] [C] [D] [E]

Numerical Reasoning

Examples

i.

0	*3*	*6*	cm²
[0]	[0]	[0]	
[1]	[1]	[1]	
[2]	[2]	[2]	
[3]	[3]	[3]	
[4]	[4]	[4]	
[5]	[5]	[5]	
[6]	[6]	[6]	
[7]	[7]	[7]	
[8]	[8]	[8]	
[9]	[9]	[9]	

ii. [A] [B] [C] [D] [E]

Numerical Reasoning
Question

1.

[0]	[0]	[0]
[1]	[1]	[1]
[2]	[2]	[2]
[3]	[3]	[3]
[4]	[4]	[4]
[5]	[5]	[5]
[6]	[6]	[6]
[7]	[7]	[7]
[8]	[8]	[8]
[9]	[9]	[9]

5.

[0]	[0]	[0]
[1]	[1]	[1]
[2]	[2]	[2]
[3]	[3]	[3]
[4]	[4]	[4]
[5]	[5]	[5]
[6]	[6]	[6]
[7]	[7]	[7]
[8]	[8]	[8]
[9]	[9]	[9]

9.

[0]	[0]
[1]	[1]
[2]	[2]
[3]	[3]
[4]	[4]
[5]	[5]
[6]	[6]
[7]	[7]
[8]	[8]
[9]	[9]

13.

[0]	[0]	[0]
[1]	[1]	[1]
[2]	[2]	[2]
[3]	[3]	[3]
[4]	[4]	[4]
[5]	[5]	[5]
[6]	[6]	[6]
[7]	[7]	[7]
[8]	[8]	[8]
[9]	[9]	[9]

2.

		min
[0]	[0]	
[1]	[1]	
[2]	[2]	
[3]	[3]	
[4]	[4]	
[5]	[5]	
[6]	[6]	
[7]	[7]	
[8]	[8]	
[9]	[9]	

6.

£		,		
[0]	.	[0]	[0]	
[1]	.	[1]	[1]	
[2]	.	[2]	[2]	
[3]	.	[3]	[3]	
[4]	.	[4]	[4]	
[5]	.	[5]	[5]	
[6]	.	[6]	[6]	
[7]	.	[7]	[7]	
[8]	.	[8]	[8]	
[9]	.	[9]	[9]	

10.

[0]	[0]	[0]
[1]	[1]	[1]
[2]	[2]	[2]
[3]	[3]	[3]
[4]	[4]	[4]
[5]	[5]	[5]
[6]	[6]	[6]
[7]	[7]	[7]
[8]	[8]	[8]
[9]	[9]	[9]

14.

[0]	[0]	[0]
[1]	[1]	[1]
[2]	[2]	[2]
[3]	[3]	[3]
[4]	[4]	[4]
[5]	[5]	[5]
[6]	[6]	[6]
[7]	[7]	[7]
[8]	[8]	[8]
[9]	[9]	[9]

3.

[0]	[0]
[1]	[1]
[2]	[2]
[3]	[3]
[4]	[4]
[5]	[5]
[6]	[6]
[7]	[7]
[8]	[8]
[9]	[9]

7.

[0]	[0]	[0]
[1]	[1]	[1]
[2]	[2]	[2]
[3]	[3]	[3]
[4]	[4]	[4]
[5]	[5]	[5]
[6]	[6]	[6]
[7]	[7]	[7]
[8]	[8]	[8]
[9]	[9]	[9]

11.

[0]	[0]	[0]
[1]	[1]	[1]
[2]	[2]	[2]
[3]	[3]	[3]
[4]	[4]	[4]
[5]	[5]	[5]
[6]	[6]	[6]
[7]	[7]	[7]
[8]	[8]	[8]
[9]	[9]	[9]

15.

[0]	[0]	[0]
[1]	[1]	[1]
[2]	[2]	[2]
[3]	[3]	[3]
[4]	[4]	[4]
[5]	[5]	[5]
[6]	[6]	[6]
[7]	[7]	[7]
[8]	[8]	[8]
[9]	[9]	[9]

4.

[0]	[0]	[0]
[1]	[1]	[1]
[2]	[2]	[2]
[3]	[3]	[3]
[4]	[4]	[4]
[5]	[5]	[5]
[6]	[6]	[6]
[7]	[7]	[7]
[8]	[8]	[8]
[9]	[9]	[9]

8.

£		,		
[0]	.	[0]	[0]	
[1]	.	[1]	[1]	
[2]	.	[2]	[2]	
[3]	.	[3]	[3]	
[4]	.	[4]	[4]	
[5]	.	[5]	[5]	
[6]	.	[6]	[6]	
[7]	.	[7]	[7]	
[8]	.	[8]	[8]	
[9]	.	[9]	[9]	

12.

[0]	[0]	[0]
[1]	[1]	[1]
[2]	[2]	[2]
[3]	[3]	[3]
[4]	[4]	[4]
[5]	[5]	[5]
[6]	[6]	[6]
[7]	[7]	[7]
[8]	[8]	[8]
[9]	[9]	[9]

16. [A] [B] [C] [D] [E]
17. [A] [B] [C] [D] [E]
18. [A] [B] [C] [D] [E]
19. [A] [B] [C] [D] [E]
20. [A] [B] [C] [D] [E]
21. [A] [B] [C] [D] [E]
22. [A] [B] [C] [D] [E]
23. [A] [B] [C] [D] [E]
24. [A] [B] [C] [D] [E]

Instructions:

1. Check that you are marking the answer for the correct question number.
2. Mark ONE answer only for each question.
3. Mark boxes like this: [A]
4. For numerical reasoning complete both the number at the top and the boxes, as shown in the example.
5. For numerical reasoning complete all boxes so if the answer is 35 and you have three boxes, then write your answer as 035.
6. Use an HB pencil and rub out any errors thoroughly.

Comprehension
Example
i [A] [B] [C] [D] [E]

Question
1. [A] [B] [C] [D] [E]
2. [A] [B] [C] [D] [E]
3. [A] [B] [C] [D] [E]
4. [A] [B] [C] [D] [E]
5. [A] [B] [C] [D] [E]
6. [A] [B] [C] [D] [E]
7. [A] [B] [C] [D] [E]
8. [A] [B] [C] [D] [E]
9. [A] [B] [C] [D] [E]
10. [A] [B] [C] [D] [E]
11. [A] [B] [C] [D] [E]
12. [A] [B] [C] [D] [E]
13. [A] [B] [C] [D] [E]
14. [A] [B] [C] [D] [E]
15. [A] [B] [C] [D] [E]
16. [A] [B] [C] [D] [E]
17. [A] [B] [C] [D] [E]
18. [A] [B] [C] [D] [E]
19. [A] [B] [C] [D] [E]
20. [A] [B] [C] [D] [E]
21. [A] [B] [C] [D] [E]
22. [A] [B] [C] [D] [E]
23. [A] [B] [C] [D] [E]
24. [A] [B] [C] [D] [E]
25. [A] [B] [C] [D] [E]

Cloze
Example
i nicknamed [ ]
  officially [ ]
  named [ ]
  referred [ ]

Question
1. boxes [ ]
  patents [ ]
  warrants [ ]
  charters [ ]

2. plentiful [ ]
  protea [ ]
  prolific [ ]
  careful [ ]

3. everyday [ ]
  use [ ]
  clever [ ]
  producing [ ]

4. rival [ ]
  competition [ ]
  friendly [ ]
  command [ ]

5. conspiracy [ ]
  contract [ ]
  legal [ ]
  debate [ ]

6. important [ ]
  impenetrable [ ]
  impractical [ ]
  impersonal [ ]

7. slowly [ ]
  quick [ ]
  quickly [ ]
  sparingly [ ]

8. impartial [ ]
  industrial [ ]
  frivolous [ ]
  humorous [ ]

9. subspecies [ ]
  substandard [ ]
  substance [ ]
  substances [ ]

10. bright [ ]
  glow [ ]
  glowing [ ]
  fade [ ]

11. showed [ ]
  demonstrated [ ]
  convinced [ ]
  carried [ ]

12. problem [ ]
  idea [ ]
  creation [ ]
  covenant [ ]

13. cringe [ ]
  spark [ ]
  burst [ ]
  jump [ ]

14. help [ ]
  infuse [ ]
  test [ ]
  stop [ ]

15. improvised [ ]
  improved [ ]
  improve [ ]
  impoverished [ ]

Non-Verbal Reasoning

Example

i. [A] [B] [C̶] [D]

Question

1. [A] [B] [C] [D]
2. [A] [B] [C] [D]
3. [A] [B] [C] [D]
4. [A] [B] [C] [D]
5. [A] [B] [C] [D]
6. [A] [B] [C] [D]
7. [A] [B] [C] [D]
8. [A] [B] [C] [D]
9. [A] [B] [C] [D]
10. [A] [B] [C] [D]

Numerical Reasoning

Example

0	4	2	cm^2
[0̶]	[0]	[0]	
[1]	[1]	[1]	
[2]	[2]	[2̶]	
[3]	[3]	[3]	
[4]	[4̶]	[4]	
[5]	[5]	[5]	
[6]	[6]	[6]	
[7]	[7]	[7]	
[8]	[8]	[8]	
[9]	[9]	[9]	

Numerical Reasoning

Question

1.

[0]	[0]	[0]
[1]	[1]	[1]
[2]	[2]	[2]
[3]	[3]	[3]
[4]	[4]	[4]
[5]	[5]	[5]
[6]	[6]	[6]
[7]	[7]	[7]
[8]	[8]	[8]
[9]	[9]	[9]

4. cm

[0]	[0]	[0]
[1]	[1]	[1]
[2]	[2]	[2]
[3]	[3]	[3]
[4]	[4]	[4]
[5]	[5]	[5]
[6]	[6]	[6]
[7]	[7]	[7]
[8]	[8]	[8]
[9]	[9]	[9]

5c. cm

[0]	[0]	[0]
[1]	[1]	[1]
[2]	[2]	[2]
[3]	[3]	[3]
[4]	[4]	[4]
[5]	[5]	[5]
[6]	[6]	[6]
[7]	[7]	[7]
[8]	[8]	[8]
[9]	[9]	[9]

7b. miles

[0]	[0]	[0]
[1]	[1]	[1]
[2]	[2]	[2]
[3]	[3]	[3]
[4]	[4]	[4]
[5]	[5]	[5]
[6]	[6]	[6]
[7]	[7]	[7]
[8]	[8]	[8]
[9]	[9]	[9]

2.

[0]	[0]	[0]
[1]	[1]	[1]
[2]	[2]	[2]
[3]	[3]	[3]
[4]	[4]	[4]
[5]	[5]	[5]
[6]	[6]	[6]
[7]	[7]	[7]
[8]	[8]	[8]
[9]	[9]	[9]

5a. cm^2

[0]	[0]	[0]
[1]	[1]	[1]
[2]	[2]	[2]
[3]	[3]	[3]
[4]	[4]	[4]
[5]	[5]	[5]
[6]	[6]	[6]
[7]	[7]	[7]
[8]	[8]	[8]
[9]	[9]	[9]

6.

[0]	[0]	[0]
[1]	[1]	[1]
[2]	[2]	[2]
[3]	[3]	[3]
[4]	[4]	[4]
[5]	[5]	[5]
[6]	[6]	[6]
[7]	[7]	[7]
[8]	[8]	[8]
[9]	[9]	[9]

7c. ℓ

[0]	[0]	[0]
[1]	[1]	[1]
[2]	[2]	[2]
[3]	[3]	[3]
[4]	[4]	[4]
[5]	[5]	[5]
[6]	[6]	[6]
[7]	[7]	[7]
[8]	[8]	[8]
[9]	[9]	[9]

3.

[0]	[0]	[0]
[1]	[1]	[1]
[2]	[2]	[2]
[3]	[3]	[3]
[4]	[4]	[4]
[5]	[5]	[5]
[6]	[6]	[6]
[7]	[7]	[7]
[8]	[8]	[8]
[9]	[9]	[9]

5b. cm^2

[0]	[0]	[0]
[1]	[1]	[1]
[2]	[2]	[2]
[3]	[3]	[3]
[4]	[4]	[4]
[5]	[5]	[5]
[6]	[6]	[6]
[7]	[7]	[7]
[8]	[8]	[8]
[9]	[9]	[9]

7a. miles

[0]	[0]	[0]
[1]	[1]	[1]
[2]	[2]	[2]
[3]	[3]	[3]
[4]	[4]	[4]
[5]	[5]	[5]
[6]	[6]	[6]
[7]	[7]	[7]
[8]	[8]	[8]
[9]	[9]	[9]

7d. £

[0]	[0]
[1]	[1]
[2]	[2]
[3]	[3]
[4]	[4]
[5]	[5]
[6]	[6]
[7]	[7]
[8]	[8]
[9]	[9]

Set B Paper 2

Instructions:

1. Check that you are marking the answer for the correct question number.
2. Mark ONE answer only for each question.
3. Mark boxes like this: [A]
4. For numerical reasoning complete both the number at the top and the boxes, as shown in the example.
5. For numerical reasoning complete all boxes so if the answer is 35 and you have three boxes, then write your answer as 035.
6. Use an HB pencil and rub out any errors thoroughly.

Cloze

Example

i.

e	a	t
[a]	[a]	[e]
[c]	[c]	[i]
[e]	[e]	[u]
[g]	[i]	[n]
[s]	[n]	[t]

Question

1.

[a]	[c]	[g]
[e]	[g]	[h]
[i]	[n]	[n]
[o]	[p]	[s]
[y]	[t]	[t]

2.

[a]	[a]	[a]
[e]	[e]	[e]
[o]	[l]	[l]
[s]	[r]	[r]
[t]	[w]	[u]

3.

[b]	[e]	[e]
[c]	[l]	[l]
[e]	[s]	[n]
[g]	[t]	[r]
[m]	[u]	[u]

4.

[a]	[i]	[a]
[e]	[l]	[e]
[g]	[n]	[i]
[i]	[r]	[g]
[u]	[u]	[t]

5.

[c]	[e]	[a]
[k]	[h]	[e]
[n]	[i]	[i]
[s]	[w]	[o]
[t]	[y]	[u]

6.

[a]	[a]	[m]
[i]	[c]	[n]
[ ]	[e]	[r]
[ ]	[s]	[t]
[ ]	[z]	[z]

7.

[c]	[c]	[a]
[l]	[h]	[e]
[n]	[i]	[i]
[s]	[o]	[o]
[t]	[s]	[u]

8.

[a]	[a]	[a]
[e]	[c]	[c]
[i]	[d]	[i]
[o]	[e]	[s]
[u]	[t]	[t]

9.

[h]	[f]	[e]
[i]	[n]	[f]
[o]	[o]	[n]
[s]	[u]	[s]
[t]	[v]	[t]

10.

[a]	[c]	[c]
[i]	[p]	[d]
[l]	[r]	[e]
[o]	[s]	[p]
[u]	[u]	[t]

11.

[a]	[e]	[e]
[e]	[n]	[i]
[i]	[o]	[n]
[l]	[r]	[t]
[o]	[x]	[y]

12.

[a]	[a]	[l]
[d]	[i]	[m]
[e]	[o]	[n]
[i]	[n]	[t]
[o]	[u]	[u]

13.

[a]	[a]	[b]
[e]	[c]	[h]
[o]	[i]	[s]
[w]	[s]	[t]
[y]	[t]	[z]

14.

[a]	[i]	[c]
[e]	[m]	[e]
[i]	[o]	[i]
[o]	[r]	[r]
[u]	[u]	[w]

Goes with Two Groups

Example

i. adhesive [ ]   6. demand [ ]
   stick [ ]   charge [ ]
   adherent [ ]   levy [ ]
   bough [ ]   rush [ ]
                         storm [ ]

Question

1. alone [ ]   7. implement [ ]
   sole [ ]   construct [ ]
   mere [ ]   fabricate [ ]
   haddock [ ]   stone [ ]
   plaice [ ]   cobble [ ]

2. stir [ ]   8. fastener [ ]
   add [ ]   buckle [ ]
   churn [ ]   tie [ ]
   mock [ ]   crease [ ]
   rib [ ]   warp [ ]

3. animal [ ]   9. apricot [ ]
   leather [ ]   fig [ ]
   bombard [ ]   prune [ ]
   slam [ ]   day [ ]
   pelt [ ]   trip [ ]

4. plane [ ]   10. Autumn [ ]
   boat [ ]   Winter [ ]
   driver [ ]   era [ ]
   tram [ ]   season [ ]
   saw [ ]   chili [ ]

5. move [ ]   11. thought [ ]
   hold [ ]   footing [ ]
   cat [ ]   base [ ]
   wolf [ ]   ground [ ]
   bear [ ]   earth [ ]

Goes with Two Groups
Continued

12. free [ ]
    absolve [ ]
    reserve [ ]
    surplus [ ]
    spare [ ]

13. solution [ ]
    method [ ]
    composite [ ]
    compound [ ]
    tea [ ]

14. rosemary [ ]
    basil [ ]
    mint [ ]
    parsley [ ]
    yarrow [ ]

15. pile [ ]
    mass [ ]
    bulk [ ]
    clump [ ]
    cloud [ ]

16. shed [ ]
    barn [ ]
    hovel [ ]
    discard [ ]
    doff [ ]

17. fundamental [ ]
    standard [ ]
    chief [ ]
    pivotal [ ]
    staple [ ]

18. utter [ ]
    say [ ]
    voice [ ]
    absolute [ ]
    unequivocal [ ]

19. groom [ ]
    neaten [ ]
    comb [ ]
    tease [ ]
    rake [ ]

20. item [ ]
    object [ ]
    device [ ]
    entity [ ]
    condemn [ ]

Similarities
Example

i. near [ ]
    go [ ]
    depart [ ]
    arrive [—]

1. enlighten [ ]
    change [ ]
    improve [ ]
    correct [ ]

2. fair [ ]
    rationalise [ ]
    correct [ ]
    excuse [ ]

3. instigate [ ]
    conclude [ ]
    indicative [ ]
    initiate [ ]

4. eat [ ]
    table [ ]
    feast [ ]
    famine [ ]

5. river [ ]
    ocean [ ]
    dirt [ ]
    pollute [ ]

6. throw [ ]
    negative [ ]
    decline [ ]
    unable [ ]

7. ludicrous [ ]
    atrocious [ ]
    stamina [ ]
    germinate [ ]

8. daring [ ]
    laughing [ ]
    pleasing [ ]
    hopeful [ ]

9. adhesive [ ]
    harsh [ ]
    comment [ ]
    strong [ ]

10. clever [ ]
    coherent [ ]
    fatuous [ ]
    fatuitous [ ]

11. nice [ ]
    solar [ ]
    brilliant [ ]
    light [ ]

12. courage [ ]
    strength [ ]
    shrewd [ ]
    startling [ ]

13. simple [ ]
    translucent [ ]
    transparent [ ]
    opaque [ ]

14. vacate [ ]
    airtight [ ]
    tenant [ ]
    haunted [ ]

15. find [ ]
    ailing [ ]
    assist [ ]
    wrought [ ]

16. flour [ ]
    flourish [ ]
    garnish [ ]
    plume [ ]

17. fear [ ]
    crazy [ ]
    temperate [ ]
    distraught [ ]

18. judgement [ ]
    inattention [ ]
    omission [ ]
    concern [ ]

19. caesura [ ]
    allusion [ ]
    append [ ]
    unfavourable [ ]

20. infant [ ]
    yielding [ ]
    adamant [ ]
    barricade [ ]

Non-Verbal Reasoning
Example

i. [A] [B] [C] [D] [E]
ii. [A] [B] [C] [D]

Question

1. [A] [B] [C] [D] [E]
2. [A] [B] [C] [D] [E]
3. [A] [B] [C] [D] [E]
4. [A] [B] [C] [D] [E]
5. [A] [B] [C] [D] [E]
6. [A] [B] [C] [D] [E]
7. [A] [B] [C] [D] [E]
8. [A] [B] [C] [D] [E]
9. [A] [B] [C] [D] [E]
10. [A] [B] [C] [D] [E]
11. [A] [B] [C] [D]
12. [A] [B] [C] [D]
13. [A] [B] [C] [D]
14. [A] [B] [C] [D]
15. [A] [B] [C] [D]
16. [A] [B] [C] [D]
17. [A] [B] [C] [D]
18. [A] [B] [C] [D]
19. [A] [B] [C] [D]
20. [A] [B] [C] [D]

Numerical Reasoning
Examples

i.

0	6	3
[0̶]	[0]	[0]
[1]	[1]	[1]
[2]	[2]	[2]
[3]	[3]	[3̶]
[4]	[4]	[4]
[5]	[5]	[5]
[6]	[6̶]	[6]
[7]	[7]	[7]
[8]	[8]	[8]
[9]	[9]	[9]

ii. [A] [B] [C] [D̶] [E]

Questions

1. [A] [B] [C] [D] [E]
2. [A] [B] [C] [D] [E]
3. [A] [B] [C] [D] [E]
4. [A] [B] [C] [D] [E]
5. [A] [B] [C] [D] [E]
6. [A] [B] [C] [D] [E]

7.

[0]	[0]	[0]
[1]	[1]	[1]
[2]	[2]	[2]
[3]	[3]	[3]
[4]	[4]	[4]
[5]	[5]	[5]
[6]	[6]	[6]
[7]	[7]	[7]
[8]	[8]	[8]
[9]	[9]	[9]

8.

[0]	[0]	[0]	[0]
[1]	[1]	[1]	[1]
[2]	[2]	[2]	[2]
[3]	[3]	[3]	[3]
[4]	[4]	[4]	[4]
[5]	[5]	[5]	[5]
[6]	[6]	[6]	[6]
[7]	[7]	[7]	[7]
[8]	[8]	[8]	[8]
[9]	[9]	[9]	[9]

9.

[0]	[0]	[0]
[1]	[1]	[1]
[2]	[2]	[2]
[3]	[3]	[3]
[4]	[4]	[4]
[5]	[5]	[5]
[6]	[6]	[6]
[7]	[7]	[7]
[8]	[8]	[8]
[9]	[9]	[9]

10.

		.	km
[0]	[0]	.	[0]
[1]	[1]	.	[1]
[2]	[2]	.	[2]
[3]	[3]	.	[3]
[4]	[4]	.	[4]
[5]	[5]	.	[5]
[6]	[6]	.	[6]
[7]	[7]	.	[7]
[8]	[8]	.	[8]
[9]	[9]	.	[9]

11.

[0]	[0]	[0]
[1]	[1]	[1]
[2]	[2]	[2]
[3]	[3]	[3]
[4]	[4]	[4]
[5]	[5]	[5]
[6]	[6]	[6]
[7]	[7]	[7]
[8]	[8]	[8]
[9]	[9]	[9]

12.

£

	.		
[0]	.	[0]	[0]
[1]	.	[1]	[1]
[2]	.	[2]	[2]
[3]	.	[3]	[3]
[4]	.	[4]	[4]
[5]	.	[5]	[5]
[6]	.	[6]	[6]
[7]	.	[7]	[7]
[8]	.	[8]	[8]
[9]	.	[9]	[9]

13.

£

[0]	[0]
[1]	[1]
[2]	[2]
[3]	[3]
[4]	[4]
[5]	[5]
[6]	[6]
[7]	[7]
[8]	[8]
[9]	[9]

14.

			s
[0]	[0]	[0]	
[1]	[1]	[1]	
[2]	[2]	[2]	
[3]	[3]	[3]	
[4]	[4]	[4]	
[5]	[5]	[5]	
[6]	[6]	[6]	
[7]	[7]	[7]	
[8]	[8]	[8]	
[9]	[9]	[9]	

15.

	.			h
[0]	.	[0]	[0]	
[1]	.	[1]	[1]	
[2]	.	[2]	[2]	
[3]	.	[3]	[3]	
[4]	.	[4]	[4]	
[5]	.	[5]	[5]	
[6]	.	[6]	[6]	
[7]	.	[7]	[7]	
[8]	.	[8]	[8]	
[9]	.	[9]	[9]	

16.

£

[0]	[0]
[1]	[1]
[2]	[2]
[3]	[3]
[4]	[4]
[5]	[5]
[6]	[6]
[7]	[7]
[8]	[8]
[9]	[9]

17.

cm^2

[0]	[0]
[1]	[1]
[2]	[2]
[3]	[3]
[4]	[4]
[5]	[5]
[6]	[6]
[7]	[7]
[8]	[8]
[9]	[9]

18.

[0]	[0]	[0]
[1]	[1]	[1]
[2]	[2]	[2]
[3]	[3]	[3]
[4]	[4]	[4]
[5]	[5]	[5]
[6]	[6]	[6]
[7]	[7]	[7]
[8]	[8]	[8]
[9]	[9]	[9]

19.

%

[0]	[0]	[0]
[1]	[1]	[1]
[2]	[2]	[2]
[3]	[3]	[3]
[4]	[4]	[4]
[5]	[5]	[5]
[6]	[6]	[6]
[7]	[7]	[7]
[8]	[8]	[8]
[9]	[9]	[9]

20.

kg

[0]	[0]
[1]	[1]
[2]	[2]
[3]	[3]
[4]	[4]
[5]	[5]
[6]	[6]
[7]	[7]
[8]	[8]
[9]	[9]

11+ C.E.M. Style Test – Pack 1 Answers

Set A Paper 1

Section 1: Comprehension

1. B. It is not A as the first sentence it is referred to as infamous as the site of a detention centre. Is not C as the Red Crab migration is the natural wonder of the world, not the island itself. It is not D as the passage gives many reasons why the island is significant such as the many unique plants and animals. The answer is B as while it is the location of a detention centre it also has many natural wonders.
2. A. See paragraph 3
3. B. Paragraph 4 compares endemic animals species to unique species of plants.
4. A. With millions of them, their habitat including domestic gardens, and their migration being a natural wonder of the world, they are clearly able to be seen.
5. B. It cannot be A because it is located south of Indonesia, and north-west of Australia; that is in the Southern Hemisphere, nowhere near the North Pole. It is not C as elves do not exist. It is not D as all the mammals on the island are small. The Island was indeed discovered on Christmas Day. While the article does not comment on this, it remains a possible reason from the article.
6. C. Provides information on a subject, in a factual manner.
7. A. An invertebrate is an animal without a backbone.
8. B. Diversity means a range of different things.

Section 2: Verbal Activity

1.	ORA	full word is laboratories
2.	HES	full word is adhesive
3.	CI,AL	full word is accidentally
4.	SAB	full word is reusable
5.	HOI	full word is choir
6.	UME	full word is consumer
7.	Japan	all of the others are in Europe
8.	Potato	this is a vegetable not a fruit
9.	Gecko	this is a reptile not a mammal
10.	Plain	all the rest are modes of transport (Plane is a type of transport but not plain)
11.	Stingy	all the rest mean 'dirty'
12.	Demolish	all the rest mean to become smaller
13.	Pledge	all the rest are awards
14.	Husky	all the rest mean strict
15.	Composer	all the rest are types of music
16.	Hear	all the rest are anagrams (contain the same letters)

Section 3: Non-Verbal Ability

1. A. two long, four small
2. C. one lone, 2 medium, two small
3. D. two long, three small
4. A. three long, two small

5. D
6. E
7. C

Section 4: Cubes

1. B
2. C
3. A
4. B
5. A
6. D
7. B
8. C
9. A
10. D

Section 5: Numerical Reasoning

1. 679
2. 326
3. 200
4. 1.75 kg (1¾ kg)
5. 17 minutes (arrives at train station at 8:05a.m.)
6. 8:00a.m. (the lowest common multiple of 3, 5 and 8 is 120)
7. 16 (to determine the average add up all the numbers, which gives 64 and then divide by how many numbers there are, which is 4)
8. 26 (the total number of pens is now 18 times 5, which is 90)
9. 20g (each side must add up to 90g)
10. 25 (cannot have part of a coach, 24 is not quite enough)
11. 36 cm² (each side is 6cm)
12. £6 (The factory uses twice as much lead as copper. Uses 2kg of copper so 4kg of lead)

Section 1: Comprehension

1. C   Watercolour, gouache and acrylic (it tells the reader in the third paragraph that gouache is a type of paint).
2. C   Depressing, as so many do not have clean water, but uplifting as the images show the "generosity and resilience of the human spirit."
3. E   It is advertising the art show.
4. B   It is where she studied painting and then "she opened her own studio".
5. D   She went to the national College of Art and Design in Dublin.
6. A   She is a local artist so must live in the local area. The Art Show is in Slough.
7. A   It is an abstract noun.

Section 2: Verbal Ability

1. A, OM   the word is random
2. CEI   the word is ceiling
3. S, ARS   the word is scarce
4. ANE   the word is sane
5. F, SY   the word is fantasy
6. R, EA   the word is release
7. C, FL   the word is conflict
8. S, NE   the word is serene
9. IMI   the word is timid
10. ACT   the word is tactful
11. EAC   the word is bleach
12. T, ER   the word is latter
13. HU, B   the word is humble
14. C, UP   the word is corrupt

15. DAY   It is good to practice the piano everyday.
16. TO   Singing hurts my sore throat.
17. TIMES   You should brush your teeth twice everyday.
18. DAY   The weather forecast said it would be hot.
19. WAS   Paris is the capital of France.
20. TO   The late frost caused crops not to grow well.
21. TIMETABLE   On the bus, she always stood up for elderly people.
22. ON   Classification is sorting things into groups.
23. LIKES   Treat others as you would like to be treated.
24. IT   The Earth rotates around the Sun once every year.
25. HE   The speech was long and monotonous.
26. HOLIDAYS   It was a beautiful day so they decided to go for a walk
27. CHECKOUTS   He applied for a part-time job at the local shop.
28. DAY   Many people keep a journal or diary.

29. NIGHT   It snowed heavily causing hazardous driving conditions.

30. BUY   He ran to the shops just before closing time.

Section 3: Non-Verbal Reasoning

1. D. arrow points clockwise, moves around square anticlockwise, triangle moves vertically on right hand side of square.
2. D. inside shape becomes outside shape.
3. E. Circle is left, left, right, right, left; pentagon is a grey, black, white repeating pattern
4. C. Length of arrow at bottom is long, medium, short repeating pattern; other shape always circle.
5. A. rotating clockwise.
6. D. Each type of arrowhead repeated twice; number of sides increases by one, arrow swaps direction.
7. C. Shape with wavy line disappears. Next shape to disappear becomes wavy.
8. B. circle, pentagon, rhombus repeating pattern; every second shape has a chevron inside.
9. B. Square fill alternates right and left; grey fill rotates anticlockwise.
10. D. Triangles – 3, 2, 2, 1, 1; hearts – 2, 2, 1, 1, 0; diamonds – 0, 1, 1, 2, 2; circles – 0, 0, 1, 1, 2

11. C. Only one where lines from both sides meet.
12. C. Not a rotation; three short lines, not two.
13. D. Three sides difference between outside and inside shapes, not two.
14. B. Small inside shape has three sides not four.
15. D. Shape not regular.
16. B. Arrow points to square, not away.
17. E. Overlap is not a triangle.
18. D. Arrow points anticlockwise, not clockwise.
19. D. Outside shape not a rotation
20. B. Inside lines do not meet at edge of shape; four sections not three.

Section 4: Numerical Reasoning

1. 57   171÷3=57
2. 31min
3. 28
4. 60mph
5. 570
6. 1.41
7. 180
8. £8.40
9. 16
10. 251
11. 952
12. 12
13. 18
14. 4
15. 167
16. A
17. C
18. E
19. C
20. B   322 x 2 = 644 and 6÷3=2
21. B   1kg = 1000g
22. D   9-(-4) = 13
23. D
24. 4

Section 1: Comprehension

1. C   line 2
2. D   lines 6-7
3. D   lines 25-26 (weekly is a little less than £6. So £6 x 50 gives approximate annual income)
4. C   lines 13-15
5. D   line 8
6. D   lines 31-32
7. A   lines 33-40
8. A   line 21
9. E   lines 46-49
10. B   lines 49-50
11. C   lines 6-7
12. C
13. B   lines 31-42, no negative views expressed
14. C   lines 13-14
15. B   This then explains the need for Fairtrade in the fourth paragraph
16. E   not mentioned anywhere in text
17. E   lines 1-4
18. D   lines 20-30
19. D   fermentation is the process where bacteria and yeast release energy without using oxygen.
20. A   exported means to send or transport to another country for sale
21. C   exploited means to make use of in an unfair way
22. D   lines 13-14. The pods cannot be mechanically picked
23. E   Describes a verb (it is not describing the chocolate)
24. E   Describes the noun (cocoa pods)
25. A   They are people / things

Section 2: Cloze

1. patents
2. prolific
3. use
4. rival
5. debate
6. impractical
7. quickly
8. industrial
9. substances
10. glow
11. demonstrated
12. problem

13. burst
14. stop
15. improved

Section 3: Non-Verbal Reasoning

1. C
2. C
3. D
4. D
5. B
6. D
7. A
8. D
9. B
10. A

Section 4: Numerical Reasoning

1. 12
2. 20
3. 92
4. 24 cm
5.   a. 16 cm^2
    b. 100 cm^2
    c. 42 cm
6. 25
7.   a. 215 miles
    b. 15 miles
    c. 23 litres
    d. £30

Section 1: Cloze

1. YTH   The word is MYTHS
2. TEL   The word is CONSTELLATIONS
3. BLE   The word is ENABLED
4. ULA   The word is REGULATE
5. CIE   The word is ANCIENT
6. ASM   The word is PLASMA
7. SIO   The word is FUSION
8. EAC   The word is REACTIONS
9. ION   The word is EXPLOSION
10. OUP   The word is COUPLE
11. AXY   The word is GALAXY
12. IAT   The word is RADIATES
13. ASH   The word is SQUASHED
14. UOR   The word is FLUORESCE

Section 2: Goes with two groups

1. sole
2. stir
3. pelt
4. plane
5. bear
6. charge
7. cobble
8. buckle
9. prune
10. season
11. ground
12. spare
13. solution
14. mint
15. mass
16. shed
17. staple
18. utter
19. comb
20. object

Section 3: Similiarities

1. improve
2. rationalise
3. initiate
4. feast
5. pollute
6. decline
7. ludicrous
8. hopeful
9. harsh
10. coherent
11. brilliant
12. shrewd
13. transparent
14. vacate
15. assist
16. flourish
17. distraught
18. judgement
19. unfavourable
20. adamant

Section 4: Non-Verbal Reasoning

1. C
2. C
3. D
4. A
5. C
6. B
7. D
8. B
9. A
10. D
11. B
12. B
13. B
14. C
15. B
16. D
17. A
18. A
19. C
20. B

Section 5: Numerical Reasoning

1. D
2. E
3. E
4. C
5. D
6. C
7. 14
8. 3185
9. 152
10. 2.7km
11. 10
12. £4.13
13. £10
14. 15s
15. 7.75 hours
16. £57
17. 36cm^2
18. 31
19. 60%
20. 11kg

Printed in Great Britain
by Amazon